Job Interview

Conquering the Job Interview Process to Be Hired by Advanced Techniques & Winning Answers

(Techniques to Overcome Anxiety and Have Amazing Body Language While Answering Questions)

Stephen Traynor

Published by Rob Miles

Stephen Traynor

All Rights Reserved

Job Interview: Conquering the Job Interview Process to Be Hired by Advanced Techniques & Winning Answers (Techniques to Overcome Anxiety and Have Amazing Body Language While Answering Questions)

ISBN 978-1-989990-69-8

All rights reserved. No part of this guide may be reproduced in any form without permission in writing from the publisher except in the case of brief quotations embodied in critical articles or reviews.

Legal & Disclaimer

The information contained in this book is not designed to replace or take the place of any form of medicine or professional medical advice. The information in this book has been provided for educational and entertainment purposes only.

The information contained in this book has been compiled from sources deemed reliable, and it is accurate to the best of the Author's knowledge; however, the Author cannot guarantee its accuracy and validity and cannot be held liable for any errors or omissions. Changes are periodically made to this book. You must consult your doctor or get professional medical advice before using any of the suggested remedies, techniques, or information in this book.

Upon using the information contained in this book, you agree to hold harmless the Author from and against any damages, costs, and expenses, including any legal fees potentially resulting from the application of any of the information provided by this guide. This disclaimer applies to any damages or injury caused by the use and application, whether directly or indirectly, of any advice or information presented, whether for breach of contract, tort, negligence, personal injury, criminal intent, or under any other cause of action.

You agree to accept all risks of using the information presented inside this book. You need to consult a professional medical practitioner in order to ensure you are both able and healthy enough to participate in this program.

Table of Contents

INTRODUCTION 1

CHAPTER 1: WHAT IS THE INTERVIEW PROCESS? 4

CHAPTER 2: DRESS CODE: CHOOSING THE RIGHT OUTFIT 15

CHAPTER 3: JOB INTERVIEWS ARE STRESSFUL 23

CHAPTER 4: BEFORE THE INTERVIEW............................... 31

CHAPTER 5: TELL ME ABOUT YOURSELF 50

CHAPTER 6: MANAGE THE INTERVIEW FOR SUCCESS 57

CHAPTER 7: KNOW WHAT YOU'RE CAPABLE OF 65

CHAPTER 8: TYPES OF INTERVIEW QUESTIONS................ 70

CHAPTER 9: HOW TO HANDLE DIFFERENT TYPES OF INTERVIEWS AND HOW TO BE SUCCESSFUL IN EACH ONE 74

CHAPTER 10: ANTICIPATING THE QUESTIONS.................. 83

CHAPTER 11: COMMON QUESTIONS AND ANSWERS 91

CHAPTER 12: TELL ME SOMETHING ABOUT YOURSELF.. 101

CHAPTER 13: PREPARING FOR A JOB HUNT 108

CHAPTER 14: QUESTIONS TO HELP YOU FIND YOUR DREAM CAREER... 115

CHAPTER 15: WE WILL CALL YOU................................... 121

CHAPTER 16: MANAGING THIRD-PARTY RECRUITERS.... 125

CHAPTER 17: GETTING TO THE INTRODUCTIONS........... 138

CHAPTER 18: GENERAL CULTURE QUESTIONS 153

CHAPTER 19: DURING THE INTERVIEW: COMMON QUESTIONS PART 2 170

CHAPTER 20: QUESTIONS EMPLOYERS ASK 182

CHAPTER 21: KNOW ABOUT BENEFITS 185

CHAPTER 22: GENERAL ADVICE 195

CONCLUSION.. 204

Introduction

Are you preparing for an upcoming interview for that dream job? Are you worried about not being well prepared for it? Or are you simply just bored of your current work and want a new job for a change? Well, you are not alone!

There are literally hundreds of thousands of people who are on the hunt for a new job every single day. To many, finding a new job can be one of the most stressful occasions in your working life. It can be tiring and mentally challenging. Your confidence can take a bashing if you do not experience early success.

More often than not, the most challenging obstacle standing between you and that job is the interview! As nerve wrecking and stressful they are, interviews play a key role in determining whether the company and candidate will make an effective match. As such, the interviewing process provides a great deal of value for the company and candidate alike.

Unlike most books, "Acing Interviews" will not simply throw you one thousand sample questions and answers to study and leave you with that (they only serve to confuse you and overload your memory with too much information. Besides, do you really want to memorize 1001 questions and the answers to each one of them?).

Instead, you will be taught step by step on how to nail that interview to land your dream job. These are actionable tips and ways which will prepare you both physically and mentally for the interview process. You will learn how to create great first impressions, stay composed and stand on your feet to give great responses. You will also be taught on how to best present yourself in a way which will make you stand out from the crowd and be noticed.

If this sounds good to you, let us dive in and start acing those interviews!

Chapter 1: What Is The Interview Process?

The interview process is a multi-stage process for hiring new employees. The interview process typically includes the following steps: writing a job description, posting a job, scheduling interviews, conducting preliminary interviews, conducting in-person interviews, following up with candidates, and making a hire.

Steps in the Job Interview Process

It's not always quick and easy to get hired. The job interview process can be lengthy. Being interviewed once and getting a job offer is typically a thing of the past. Today, many companies have an involved interview process starting with screening interviews, which often take place on the phone, followed by in-person interviews, second interviews, and even third interviews.

In addition to a hiring manager, you make meet with managers, employees, and other staff. How hiring is handled depends on the employer and the systems they have in place for screening and evaluating potential new hires. Here's an overview of each step in the interview process, along with advice on the best way to handle each type of interview as you progress up the interview ladder towards a job offer.

Screening Interview

A screening interview is a type of job interview that is conducted to determine if the applicant has the qualifications needed to do the job for which the company is hiring. A screening interview is typically the first interview in the hiring process if the company does not start with open interviews where multiple candidates are screened at an open hiring event.

Phone Interview

Employers use phone interviews to identify and recruit candidates for employment. Phone interviews are often used to narrow the pool of applicants who will be invited for in-person interviews. For remote jobs, interviewing by phone, Skype, or video may be how you get hired.

First Interview

The first in-person job interview is typically a one-on-one interview between the applicant and a hiring manager. The interviewer will ask questions about the applicant's experience and skills, work history, availability, and the qualifications the company is seeking in the optimal candidate for the job.

Second Interview

A second interview can be a more in-depth one-on-one interview with the person you initially interviewed with, or it can be a day-long interview that includes meetings with company staff. You may meet with management, staff members, executives, and other company employees. Once you're scheduled for a second interview, you're most likely in serious contention for the job.

Third Interview

When you have made it through the first interview, then a second interview, you might think you're done with the interview process, and you'll soon find out whether you'll be receiving a job offer. That's not necessarily the case. You may have to participate in a third interview and possible more interviews after that. A third interview typically involves a final meeting with the hiring manager and may provide the opportunity to meet more of your prospective colleagues.

Dining Interview

Dining with job applicants allows employers to review your communication and interpersonal skills, as well as your table manners, in a more relaxed (for them) environment. Depending on the interview process of the company you're interviewing with, and the type of job you are applying for, you may be invited to a lunch or dinner interview.

Final Interview

The final interview is the last step in the interview process and the interview where you may find out whether or not you are going to get a job offer. Here's information on preparing for an interview when you have already met with the company multiple times, and advice on how to handle a final interview.

Review Interview Questions and Answers

Regardless of where you are in the interview process, it's important to practice interviewing and to be prepared for the typical interview questions you'll be asked during each step in the process. It's also important to have questions ready to ask the interviewer.

Follow Up After Each Step in the Interview Process

Even though it may seem like a lot of work, especially when you have gone to multiple interviews, it's essential to follow up after each step in the interview process. The most important thing you can do is to follow up and reiterate your interest in the position and to thank the interviewer for taking the time to meet with you.

Background Check

You may receive a job offer contingent on a background check and a credit check. Or, a background check may be conducted before a company offering a job. What the company learns during the background check could result in you not getting a job offer or in the job offer being withdrawn.

Job Offer

When you have made it through the sometimes grueling interview process, the final step will be a job offer. The job offer may have conditions attached, so review the terms carefully. Before you accept, it's essential to evaluate the compensation package, consider whether you want to make a counteroffer, and then accept (or decline) the job offer in writing.

Seven Phases of the Job Interview Process

Job interviews provide opportunities for job applicants to sell themselves to potential employers. Job applicants need to invest their time in preparing for the interview and understanding the interview process. Seven different phases comprise the complete job interview process. The job applicant should understand the purpose of each phase and how to make the best impression.

Preparation

The preparation phase comes before the actual job interview and requires the most substantial time investment by the job applicant. The job applicant needs to research the company's history and values, review potential questions that might be asked, choose an outfit to wear, and locate the company on a map. The applicant should ask a friend to role-play the interview. This allows the applicant to rehearse and become comfortable with the interview process.

Greeting

The interview begins with the greeting phase. The job applicant greets every person she meets that day. This includes the receptionist as well as the interviewers. As the job applicant greets each individual, she should shake the other person's hand, look him in the eye and introduce herself. This introduction needs to include the applicant's name and the name of the person with whom she is meeting.

Rapport

After the greeting phase, the job applicant enters the rapport phase. During this phase, the job applicant establishes rapport with each person she meets. Establishing rapport allows her to build a relationship with the other person and allows the other person to remember her favorably after the interview ends. The applicant should note specific items around the office that she could talk about to establish that rapport. These items might include a picture of a champion sports team or a professional award. After she identifies one of these items, she should comment favorably on the item. For example, she might state that the sports team played well last season or offer congratulations on the award.

Information Gathering

The interview then moves into the information-gathering phase. The applicant uses this phase to gather information about the company, such as markets where the company operates, potential opportunities, or what the company culture is like. The interviewer collects information regarding the applicant, such as her professionalism, her qualifications, and her ability to fit with the company.

Sell Yourself

The interview also includes a selling phase. During the selling phase, the applicant sells herself to the interviewer. She talks about the way that her qualifications match the needs of the company. She also shares any opportunities she sees and how she can contribute to the company.

Close

The closing phase ends the physical interview. During this phase, the applicant requests business cards from the interviewer and expresses her interest in the job. She shakes hands with the interviewer. She also asks the interviewer about the next steps in the hiring process.

Follow Up

When the applicant leaves the physical interview, the follow-up phase begins. The applicant enters this phase by writing notes about the interview that took place. These notes include specific information about the job or the needs of the interviewer. When the applicant arrives back home, she pulls out these notes and writes thank-you letters to each person she met at the interview. She should include a sentence that applies to the specific conversation she had with the interviewer. By referring to her notes, she can remember what they discussed.

Chapter 2: Dress Code: Choosing The Right Outfit

Unless you're applying for a job in the fashion industry, this bit can get complicated for the beginner. Different companies have different interpretations of various dress codes. There are also companies that aren't really picky when it comes to what you wear to your interview; but that doesn't mean you can take your choice of clothes lightly. You will always want to dress the part.

Fortunately, you only have to understand two big concepts when it comes to dressing the part: smart casual and business formal.

Smart Casual

As the name implies, this isn't as heavy as full coats-and-ties approaches. You can usually see these dress codes at technology firms and more modern businesses with younger owners.

Men

For men, this could mean something in between silk long-sleeve shirts or comfortable button-up short sleeves. Don't try to get too comfortable with a polo-shirt. You definitely do not want to do that. Ties are optional in these case. When it comes to shirt colors, try to go with something with a hint of purple or pink or red.

The reason behind this choice of color has an added advantage to your chances of getting the job. Studies have shown that people presenting themselves with the said colors come off as more convincing and confident as compared to people not sporting those colors.

As for bottoms, jeans are alright, but don't take it too far. You will want to use a very nice pair of jeans without any designs or prints or rips. You're not there to make a fashion statement. You will want to look as clean and crisp as possible. In order to achieve that effect, couple your jeans with a good black leather belt. Do not forget to tuck your shirt in for a more formal effect.

When it comes to shoes, some companies allow their employees to wear rubber shoes to work. As an applicant, you do not have the luxury of assuming that they will allow you to do the same. Remember that you're there for a business meeting regarding your employment with them. Your best bet here are black leather shoes.

If those clash with your shirt, try leather boat shoes in brown or white. They may not look as formal as black leather shoes, but they certainly won't make you look too casual for your formal job interview.

Women

Smart casual allows women to take a step back when it comes to their overall wardrobe. You don't necessarily have to wear a full formal dress but you don't want to look too shabby either. A simple work blouse for tops will work very well in this case. The same color scheme with the men's section also helps.

More importantly, if you intend to wear a sleeveless blouse to your interview, do not forget to couple that with a dark-colored blazer or coat to complete your corporate look.

Interestingly, your choice of undergarments will also matter at this point. Do not pick an upper undergarment that has a bright color. This might show from underneath your blouse and create a distracting image that might throw off your interviewer.

For bottoms, jeans are alright as well. Make sure they don't have any rips or designs to make it as appropriate for work as possible. Skirts are also alright as long as they aren't too short. Your indicator here is one inch above the knee. Anything that goes higher than that will show them that you're going to a party instead of an interview.

When it comes to shoes, closed-toe pointed shoes will do just fine. You don't necessarily have to take out the heels during your first interview but it never hurts to do so. Try to avoid fancy gladiator sandals or sneakers and the like. Something slick and formal will do.

Business Formal

This modus is for those who really want to make an impression. You can expect to be asked to come in this theme especially when you're applying for a high-paying, high-difficulty job. This is where you take out all the stops and ensure that you get the job.

Men

Never go short sleeve here even if you plan on wearing a coat or a suit. You will always want to wear a long-sleeved polo to go well with your suit. A good, solid, white colored polo will do since it will be covered mostly by your choice of suit.

Make sure that your slacks match your suit. Nothing could be more embarrassing than to see a mismatch. This is why choosing the right-colored suit can be confusing. With plenty of fabrics and colors and patterns to choose from, it's hard to tell what would look good in a business setting.

To make matters easy, forget about colors and patterns and just go with plain black. You can never go wrong with a sleek, black suit. It is a very powerful color that shows them that you want to be taken seriously without trying too hard.

For shoes, never ever wear anything else except black leather shoes. These are the only things that go well with a black suit.

Women

You can go one of two ways here. You can either go for a full-scale business dress or a two-piece blouse and slacks combination to make the best impression.

If you're going for a dress, again, black is the best way to go. It's chic and shows your interviewer that you want to look good and to be taken seriously as well. Just don't forget the earlier rule about skirt lengths. You don't want to go too short and look like you're there for something besides work.

You also don't want too many patterns, designs, ruffles and slits in your dress. Although these may look good, they don't add any professionalism to your image.

Accessories

You don't want to put on too much distracting ornaments on yourself as this will also distract your interviewer. Less is more in this case.

For men, wearing a watch helps the image but don't go any further than that. If you have earrings, it would be a good idea not to wear them to your interview. Wedding rings are alright, but anything more than that would be a distraction.

For the ladies, earrings are alright as long as they're not too large. Studs are the best way to go. Bracelets and bangles should be kept to a minimum, though. The same can be said about rings. Large, gaudy necklaces are meant for parties and not interviews so those should stay in the jewelry box for the meantime.

The General Idea

Your main approach here is to look like someone who should be taken seriously. This is why a direct and simple approach is the best way to go. It shows them that you want to be professional and that you would look good while working hard. You'll have plenty of time to mix and match your outfits when you get the job so don't put too much thought into your interview wardrobe.

Chapter 3: Job Interviews Are Stressful

In this book I have listed some advice for dealing with both a basic interview and a group or panel interview. I have also listed a few question examples you can expect to be asked during your interview process.

Having an idea of questions to expect ahead of time will help you prepare to have an answer ready. Can you picture this? There is nothing worse than being nervous, then asked a question, to find yourself sitting quietly. Feeling duh, ... I don't know... I never thought about that before... Did you imagine it? I bet it didn't look pretty. Not what you want to happen during your interview process is it? So, keep reading and learning.

By reading these questions in preparation for your interview and coming up with answers before your interview you will not be caught off guard. This will help you answer with confidence and show your professionalism despite the fact your nerves are making your insides quake.

Unless of course you are one of those rare people that don't get nervous under pressure or at interviews. If that describes you consider me impressed. I wish I could be more like that but I'm not, so I use these practice techniques listed in my book.

Myself, I get nervous. I started research about job interviewing to prepare for a job promotion I wanted for myself. While there was quite a bit of information out there online about this subject, I thought to myself I wish it was condensed in one book. Then I wouldn't have had to hop around online. One website after the other. That would save me time and confusion.

After my research as I prepared for my interview, it came to me it should be in a simple to understand and relate to book. I am going to put this type of book together to help people like me ace their interviews! Short and to the point.

Job interviews are stressful to most people. Learning the skills and tips I am going to share with you in this book will help you to hopefully take the stress out of your interview process.

There are several types of interviews employers and businesses use. The style used usually depends on the size of the company or business you are interviewing with.

Always bring a copy of your resume with you. Even if you attached your resume to an online application. This way the person conducting the interview can make notes on it. Of course, they may not make any notations, but it will be a reminder later sitting on their desk after they finish all the interviews lined up in addition to yours. Keeping your name fresh in their memory. Helping you to stand out from the crowd.

I know, I know, most of you don't like being the center of attention or standing out in a crowd, but this is the one time you want to stand out. You don't have to be obnoxious to stand out. Using little touches like leaving a copy of your resume. Maybe bring more than one copy just in case you end up in a group interview, more about group interviews as you read Chapter two.

Introduce yourself, make eye contact and at the end thank them for their time. This way you show professional manners.

There are different styles of interviews. You may not know until you walk in the room which one is going to happen during your interview. Read about the different styles of interviews, in the chapter "Interview styles" to be ready for whatever card you draw. With preparation and a bit of luck you can win the interview game.

You can practice answering the interview questions I have written in the chapter "Top interview questions" in front of a mirror or better yet, have a friend or family member role play them with you. By practicing, when you are in the real interview your memory will automatically reach for the practiced answer. You'll be less likely to freeze up on the spot trying to struggle to come up with the answer. Then if you feel the freeze, and struggle, panic rises, and then you'll feel like you blew it.

Don't give up even if that happens remember at one time every one of those people interviewing you were in your shoes. Smile and own it. Maybe say "Wow, I know I shouldn't be nervous, but I really would like this job, so I am nervous, lets' try that again." This will give you a minute to regroup and remind them how it feels to be on your side of the desk or table. Bottom line we are all human.

When you feel like stopping, think about why you started. Why you want this job. That will motivate you to keep going and ace your interview. Try to think of this interview as a conversation not a grill me session. Keep it flowing naturally, getting to know each other.

The supervisor getting to know you and yes, even you getting to know them. It may be after the interview you decide it's not the right company or job for you. So, this is interview isn't just about you being evaluated. You're also checking out the company or business to see if it is a good fit for you. Does it feel welcoming? Do the other employees look happy or just stressed out? Look around while you are waiting. Pay attention to little details.

Remember nobody will just give you a job or promotion. It takes preparation, hard work and most of all a belief in yourself that you deserve it and can do it. If you don't believe in yourself why should anyone else.

Each day is a chance for a new beginning. So, if you didn't get the last job you aimed for, that doesn't mean you won't ace this try at interviewing for that coveted job.

It's time to make a change, all change must start with you wanting it. That's true for job interviews, or stopping smoking, learning to dance, anything in life. If you want it, you can have it by putting the time and effort into learning how to do it. Just go for it. I didn't have a clue how to make a webpage. I decided I was going to make one and add affiliate marketing to earn money.

I researched how to do that, made my Bluehost word press website and in my first week earned $65.00 Since my website is new that doesn't' happen every week, but with some more work it will earn much more than that.

If you are interested in learning how to make a website, check out my page <u>relax-live-enjoy</u> read about it, then sign up with my link. Add a blue host link yourself to your website/ blog and everyone that signs up with your link will earn you money in addition to the other affiliate advertising you will add to your website. It's like a part time job itself.

I'll get on with the topic of interviews. Believe or not I am trying to keep this book short and informational. Sometimes I get sidetracked. Let's move on to Chapter two, interview styles.

Chapter 4: Before The Interview

Once your interview is scheduled, start preparing for it. There are a number of things you can do during the various phases of the interview that will make a good impression and help secure your dream job.

You should call the person the day before the interview to confirm the appointment. If you are not sure where the interviewee's office is located you can ask at this time. Plan to arrive ten minutes before the interview. Ninety percent of job openings are not advertised. You may learn about job vacancies that are not found in the newspapers or employment offices through such an interview, so prepare yourself so that you make a great impression. Choose clothing that you would wear for a usual job interview.

Things to Do Before the Job Interview

Research About the Organization and Interviewers

The interview will be smoother if you know the key information about the company. Refer to the organization's website, latest press releases, and social media articles to gain an insight into the company's goals. This can also help you decide if the job is right for you. If any questions pop up during this time, jot them down to look at in the future.

Practice Answering Common Questions

Prepare yourself for answering the most common questions and topics that are discussed in interviews. These include: "Tell us about yourself," "Why you are interested in taking up this position in our company?" and "Why are you the best candidate?" Present a positive image of yourself and talk about how you can contribute to the organization. Remember to focus on what you can do for them, not what they can do for you

Read the Job Description Carefully

You can print out the description of the job and read through it thoroughly. Underline the specific skills the employer is looking for in a candidate. Think about some things from your previous and current jobs that align with the job requirements. Try to come up with concrete examples to use in the interview.

Use the STAR Method for Answering Questions

You will almost certainly be asked to describe a previous experience where you used a specific skill, so you should be prepared to tell stories of your past work experience. Follow the STAR technique where you first describe the situation, then the task, the action you took, and the final result.

Use the Help of a Friend

Practicing is most effective when you say the answers out loud. You can either say them in front of a mirror or ask a friend to help you with the answers. In this way, you will gain confidence and be well prepared for the interview. If you do enlist the help of a friend, show them the job description and help them brainstorm potential questions for you to practice answering.

Prepare a Reference List

You may be asked to give some references prior to or after the interview. If your reference list is ready beforehand, the hiring process may move more quickly. Be sure to contact your references before submitting your list to the employer. Make sure they are willing to be a reference for you.

Keep Examples of Work Ready

You will probably be asked to show some past work you have done that is related to this job. After you have reviewed the job description, think about the work you have done in clubs, volunteer positions, or past jobs that show you are prepared for and have the experience necessary to be successful at the job.

Be Ready to Ask Smart Questions

Interviews involve a conversation between the interviewers and the interviewee, so you are expected to ask some pertinent questions to show your genuine interest in the organization and position. Be prepared to ask some smart questions to show off your skills and impress your employers.

Tips for the Day of the Interview

Plan Your Attire Beforehand

If possible, find out about the company's dress code for the workplace and dress accordingly. You can try to talk to someone who works there, or you can do some research to find an appropriate outfit. It is better to be overdressed than underdressed. Prepare your outfit the night before so you do not have to worry about clothes on the day of your interview.

Things to Take to the Interview

You should take a minimum of five printed copies of your resume if there are multiple interviewers. You can highlight some specific accomplishments in your personal copy so that you may refer to it and discuss it during the interview.

Take a notebook and pen to jot down points during the interview. These will be useful during the follow-up process.

Arrive Early

Plan your schedule so that you arrive at least ten to fifteen minutes early. If you are using public transportation, have a backup plan in case there are sudden closures or delays.

Make a Fantastic First Impression

Be careful about the little things. See to it that your shoes are shining, there are no holes or stains on your clothes, and your nails are not dirty. Dress appropriately and try to look professional. Keep a smile on your face and exhibit confidence by standing tall.

Behave in a Courteous Manner

Treat everyone with respect including the people you meet in the parking lot, at the security station, and at the front desk. The potential employer may ask them for feedback about you.

Display Positive Body Language

Walk and sit in a confident manner and keep your back straight. You can manage your anxiety and nervousness by breathing deeply and exhaling slowly. Shake hands with the interviewer and smile.

Remember the Four C's for Communication.

Clear: Ensure that the statements you make are clear. It should not be possible to interpret them in various ways.

Concise: You should be brief. You need not elaborate on things and give countless details unless it is necessary or you have been asked to do so.

Coherent: See to it that there is a flow to your statements. They should be connected in a coherent manner.

Complete: You should tell the complete story without leaving out the essential bits of information.

Be Authentic and Positive

You can win over the employers by being sincere and genuine during the conversation. Displaying positivity with good body language and a smile can help keep the interview flowing in a constructive and light direction.

Be honest about your accomplishments and skills. Do not exaggerate them, but do not undersell yourself. Focus on the key strengths you have that make you the right fit for the job. Explain the way that the strengths are related to the goal of the company or department and how they may be beneficial for the employer.

Support Your Answers with Examples

Give examples from your previous jobs where you successfully performed tasks related to this job description. Include concrete and quantifiable data to demonstrate your specific accomplishments.

Give Concise and Pertinent Answers

Do not waste time rambling. This is why it is important to practice your answers so that you can respond in an appropriate and relevant manner without taking too much time for each answer. Unless you are asked for a detailed answer, spend only two or three minutes on each answer.

Do Not Say Negative Things About Previous Employers

Organizations like to hire people who are problem solvers and can overcome difficult situations. They do not wish to hire people who cannot get along with others or have a habit of blaming others for their shortcomings. So if you criticize your previous supervisors or employers, you may not be hired. Remain as positive as possible even if your previous employer was unpleasant.

How to Prepare Yourself Psychologically

When you go for an interview, you will need to prepare. You have to prepare mentally, physically and emotionally because you have to be prepared for everything.

We are going to talk about some valuable information on the route to preparation success. The journey will encompass the practicalities such as how to get to the desired location along with important sections relating to self-assessment. Once you have accomplished all the research associated with these sections, you will now need a medium to help you to simulate the interview process so that you can see how you would fare in a situation that mimics the interview itself. Some good advice here is to prepare for the interview by asking a friend or family member to simulate the interview process with you. If this feels a little strange, you can mentally rehearse your anticipated response to expected questions instead.

Visualization of the task ahead is a powerful way of preparing yourself mentally (refer to the "Stress Busters" section to see how this works). Use breaks in your working day to your benefit by mentally rehearsing anticipated role-plays that may occur between you and the interviewer. During these rehearsals, ensure that you are complete, clear, and concise in your delivery. Visualize yourself making strong eye contact with your interviewer. Stick to the point regarding questions asked. Do not speak too quickly or too slowly and deliver information in a confident and self-assured fashion. There may be instances when you are unsure of the answer that is required. Do not bluff! Admit it when you do not know the answer. Most importantly, if you have decided to ask a friend or member of your family to conduct a mock interview ensure that you ask for their feedback. They may not be professional advice experts, but will throw up some valid points for reflection. I cannot overestimate how important the rehearsal phase is in this process and the confidence that it will breed.

Analyze the way your answers sound on your tape. You'll be able to hear little mistakes you didn't notice when you were in the midst of the mock interview. You may talk too quickly or start every answer with "Um …" On your next run-through, make a conscious effort to make yourself sound more professional. If there's no one available to help you test out your interviewing skills, enlist the help of a tape recorder and a mirror. Look and listen carefully. When you answer a question, do you look straight ahead in a confident manner? Are the pitch of your voice and the tone pleasant? Do you slur your words, or do you speak clearly and distinctively? All these things will give you plenty to work on before that eventful day when you have your first interview.

How to Acquire the Perfect Mindset

Allow Yourself to Dream

Unfortunately, most of us were educated out of dreaming. "Dreamer" was not a positive label when I was a young kid, and it isn't often associated with a positive connotation today. We are supposed to face reality to get prepared for "the world out there" and a life of hard work. So many of us unlearned the art of dreaming and visioning because of similar imposed beliefs. We suppressed our attention to our inner world in favor of the outer world, forgetting that the latter is a result of the former. Now we know that there's no plan without a vision; no reality without a dream. So let's go back to be that dreamer and dream ourselves to success.

You deserve to stand in the limelight. You are entitled to your big dream of being a famous motivational speaker, an activist that changes the world, a corporate leader who brings in more business with your presentation, or whatever your dream role is. What could this role ideally look like at tomorrow's gig? Dreaming of a successful interaction with your intended audience is one of the best ways you can prepare the night before your event.

Exercise: Dream Yourself to Success

Close your eyes. Picture the venue of your event in your mind. Now imagine your audience. They are joining you tomorrow because they are eager to hear what you have to share. They need to hear your message; they are hungry for what you have to offer. And you know you have important wisdom to share which will benefit them. They want you to succeed because they want to get the most for their time and money. This doesn't mean they want you to be perfect. They just want to get the value you can provide to them. And you can, because you are the expert in your field and you have a myriad of valuable insights to share with them. They are attending this event because they know they will walk away with value and learn something from you. And you know they will.

Step outside yourself. This is not about you. They are the ones who will benefit from your presentation and the reason why you are on stage. Take a moment to internalize this. During your talk, you let them feel that they are the reason you are there by asking questions and allowing them to participate. You make the presentation all about them, which reduces your speaking anxiety.

Take a moment to acknowledge this appreciative audience. They are hanging on each of your words as you present your content, as you share your story. It is okay to be vulnerable. As you allow yourself to be vulnerable, they connect with you deeply. You ask questions, and they are eager to participate because this topic is truly relevant to their lives and careers. See in your mind's eye how easy it is to engage and connect with them.

Some people nod in agreement during your talk; they all pay close attention to your words and your presentation. They appreciate you for doing this, for sharing your wisdom, for having the courage to be on that stage or in front of that room.

It's the end of your talk and people applaud with appreciation. You revel in that applause for a while and enjoy the feeling of a successful presentation.

Tailor this visualization as needed, adding specifics from your speaking engagement to the visualization. For the rest of the night, continue dreaming about this enjoyable event, and wake up.

To fully prepare for an interview, it is critical to identify the mind games you are playing with yourself and then counter them with clear thinking. Authenticity is the key to making meaningful connections and a crucial part of successful interviewing. Be honest in your answers, step outside your comfort zone, let go of uniformity, and dare to be the true you. Getting ready for an interview is a chain reaction of building knowledge, clarity, and confidence. As you gain understanding about a job, your strengths and qualifications naturally come to the fore.

Knowledge is power. Gather information about yourself, your target company, your industry. Go deep.

Get clear about what you can bring to the job, and the image you want to project during the interview. Determine the three top qualities you want to convey to the interviewer—these are your "three words." They are the words that you feel most connected to and would represent you at your best in this new position. Believe in what you are communicating and be confident about what you bring to the table. If you don't believe in what you're conveying, no one else will, either.

If you think deep about the answers wisely enough and practice everything through a staged mock interview with a family member or a friend, you are most likely to go through your first interview in a more confident manner.

Sit down with your best friend and have her fire some questions at you. Ask for her feedback. Do you sound assured and confident, or are your answers rambling and off the mark? Would she hire the person answering the questions? If not, you have some work to do.

Study the tough questions at the back of this book. Not all of those questions will be asked, but many will—they are basic to what your prospective employer will want to know about you. You should also be aware of questions specific to the type of job you are interviewing for. For example, if it's a position in human resources, you may be asked questions about your most successful recruitment effort and—the other side of the coin—your least successful. Be prepared to answer both.

Have a friend tape you with a video camera or use a webcam, which you may have access to through your computer. You'll get a look at yourself through the interviewer's eyes. Make sure to keep an eye on your body language, as it can tell a great deal about you. Do you slouch in your chair, or do you sit up straight and attentively? Are you able to maintain eye contact without staring? Your body language should show the interviewer that you're alert and focused—no folded arms, no crossed legs. Your hands can work against you in an interview—if you're used to talking with them, don't. Your hands belong on your lap; let your mouth do the talking.

Chapter 5: Tell Me About Yourself

"Tell me about yourself" is the most commonly used question in an interview and in most interviews it will be your first question. This question will set the tone for the rest of the interview so it is a must that you prepare properly in order to start off the interview on the right foot. If you do not prepare properly for this question, you run the risk of losing some interview point's early on.

What the interviewer is looking for?

The interviewer is looking to see how you can handle an open ended question. The last thing you want to do when being asked this question is say, "Well what do you want to know?" This will put a bad taste in the interviewer's mouth. The interviewer wants to hear about your previous work experience, education, and what led you to this point in your life. Just remember that you are trying to make an impression regarding the job you are applying for so it is important to stick to discussing how you are the best candidate for this position. Do you want your interviewer to remember you as being a highly qualified candidate for the job or do you want to be remembered for having an interest in the same football team?

How to not answer the question??

This question is not an open invitation to talk about what you did when you were a kid, where you grew up, how old your mom was when she gave birth to you or what your favorite restaurants and bars are to visit on a Saturday night. Quite frankly, the interviewer does not care about any of the above and if you start an interview talking about anything irrelevant to the job you're a candidate for, there may be a good chance your interview will be cut short. It is important to stay away from any personal information that is not relevant to the job you are interviewing for.

How to Answer the Question?

This question represents the opportunity to let the employer know that you are the right candidate for the position and you have the qualifications. This question gives you the right to brag about yourself a little bit. Don't be afraid to brag. It is your job to let the interviewer know that you are the right person for the job. When answering the "Tell me about yourself question", there should only be a couple of factors you incorporate into your answer. These include you're:

☐ Key strengths – Incorporate three to four key strengths that you've obtained at a previous job/internship or organization and how you can bring them to the job you're interviewing for. Do not be afraid to brag about yourself in an interview (think about it; the purpose of the interview is to sell yourself). When highlighting your key strengths, be sure to mention strengths that are essential to the job you're interviewing for (this is where your job research becomes essential). For an example, if the job requires leadership and communication skills, don't be afraid to mention those in your answer because these are the key skills that are going to set you apart from your competition.

☐ Recent Work Experience – The interviewer is not looking for the details of every job you've ever had. Instead, touch primarily on your most recent work experience and what you did at that job/internship that prepared you for the job you're currently interviewing for. It is also okay to lightly touch on some of your older jobs as long as you have acquired relevant skills or traits from these experiences.

☐ Accomplishments – As with your strengths, don't be afraid to brag. In fact, this question gives you the right to brag about yourself, and you should take advantage of it. Give the interviewer two or three accomplishments that you've obtained at previous job, organization or classroom. If you have no major accomplishments, talk about some of the high points in your college matriculation. If you feel as though you have no accomplishments or high points, think deeper. Consider lightly touching on your job duties and how those duties have helped you develop the skills it takes to be successful in the position you're applying for. Considering the fact that many college students and recent graduates have no prior work experience, you may want to touch on some of your college achievements. For example, did you win any academic awards, certifications, scholarships, etc.?

☐ What have you learned – Talk about what you learned at your previous jobs or organizations (ONLY if you don't have previous work experience) and how these lessons have prepared you for this position. This is your chance to show the interviewer that you learned skills that their company will admire.

Sample **Answer**

Q. Tell me about yourself?

A. Sure. Well, throughout my college matriculation I have had the opportunity to be involved in a number of social organizations, such as _____. Not only have I been a part of these organizations, I've also held office positions in those organizations, such as _____. Through each position, I have learned valuable skills that I am sure your company will value, such as leadership, diligence, dedication, multi-tasking, and the ability to work under pressure with tight deadlines. I understand that I will be faced with challenges in this position in which I will be required to overcome certain obstacles. I feel as though my work experience will allow me to complete these tasks as efficiently and timely as possible. I can give concrete examples if you'd like.

This is a perfect answer for candidates who lack work experience. In this answer, the candidate has identified his core strengths and the core values it takes to be successful in this position. It's always a good idea to tell the interviewer that you can provide more details if they would like. This indicates that you are well-prepared and that you were very active in your social organizations. 9 times out of 10 the interviewer will want to hear details, just be prepared to do so. If you lack work experience or you are a recent college grad, don't be afraid when this question arises. Keep in mind that you have the skills it takes to get hired for this position. How do I know this? You got called for an interview, right? Obviously, they saw some value in speaking with you.

Important Note: Make sure your answer is no shorter than thirty seconds but no longer than two minutes. You want to give the interviewer a brief description of your qualifications without sounding like a broken record (If the interviewer needs more details, they will ask).

Chapter 6: Manage The Interview For Success

They just called. You've got a job interview for 9 am on Monday! "I don't believe it," you say. "I thought this would never come. I've spent weeks responding to job listings, circulating my resume, writing letters, pounding the pavement, and receiving rejections as well as promising leads. This has not been my idea of a good time. But finally, my job search has paid off. If I can just do well in the interview, be my very best self, I can get this job, make good money, and enjoy the good life. But what happens if I blow it? What can I do between now and Monday to prepare?"

1.1 Success or Stress

Congratulations, you've got an interview. We hope you are on the way to a job that's right for you. You are wise to recognize the importance of the interview as well as to question what you can do to prepare. While that phone call is a sign of success, you still have hurdles to clear before you are offered the job. You need to prepare to interview for success rather than experience failure because you were unprepared.

Let's be perfectly clear about what that phone call means. You got the call and an invitation to interview because you were successful in marketing your resume, writing letters, and networking for job leads. After all, the specific goal of writing a resume, letters, and networking is to get a job interview, not a job.

The invitation to interview appears to put you closer to an actual job, but it is not a job offer, only an invitation to ask you, in person, some questions to further determine if you might fit into the organization. Remember, it's not over until you and the employer finalize the nuts-and-bolts of the employment process and offers to detail your duties, responsibilities, and negotiation of your salary and benefits. These are the most desirable outcomes of the interview process. This could be one of many invitations to interview you receive on the road to getting the job you really want. By the way, did you know you just had your first interview when you answered the phone and received the invitation to interview? That's right. You were most likely screened over the phone for what should become your next interview - a face-to-face meeting, which is the formal job interview. Congratulations, you just came through your first interview with success! Even though you have learned a great deal about yourself and others during these past few weeks of job hunting, let's face it, you are not in this for the learning experience.

Despite what all those career counselors and books say, finding a job is no fun. You put a lot of your ego on the line and risk rejection every time you make a phone call or send out a resume. Besides, you would rather be employed and making money, right? Try as we may to make the job search process upbeat and positive, the job search process seems demeaning to many people. It seems so impersonal, superficial, and detached. It appears to be a game of chance where timing and luck often seem more important in the hiring process than one's hard-earned skills and capabilities. Employers quickly screen many people and then select a few for the final selection. They don't have or take time to really get to know you. While it may be a selection process for interviewers, it's an elimination game for interviewees. You may have experienced weeks of mixed emotions.

You've seen the peaks and valleys, and it may seem that the lows have been far more prevalent than the highs. After all, you have put your ego on the line, displayed your weaknesses to strangers, collected rejections, felt frustrated, developed false expectations, and experienced disappointments. Now you are supposed to put on your best performance as you walk on the employer's stage to clearly communicate both verbally and nonverbally why the employer should hire you. Now it's on to the interview where you will probably experience the greatest stress in all of your job searches.

1.2 Old Adage

Truths! Just how ready are you for this interview? Will you interview for success? What are you going to do between now and the interview on Monday? What questions will the interviewer most likely ask you? How will you answer them? Are there certain questions you may have trouble answering, or which may reveal your weaknesses and thus disqualify you from further consideration? What additional information do you need about this employer? What questions should you ask during the interview? Is this the type of organization you really would like to work in? What will you do if you are offered a job? Are you prepared to accept the first offer presented to you, or are you planning to negotiate the best possible salary? Let's get even more specific. What are you going to wear on Monday, especially the colors, fabrics, and styles? What time will you arrive? What is the first thing you will do when you meet the interviewer face-to-face? Remember the old adage you never have a second chance to make a first impression. And that is what the interview is all about - making good first impressions.

Give me an example of a time when you made a bad decision. Got some good answers? They better be good, because these are some of the most important questions interviewers pose either directly or indirectly.

1.3 Manage Stress

We all want to be the very best we can. And if you will anticipate and prepare for the questions you can expect to be asked and fine-tune your interpersonal and communication skills; you should do your best in the crucial job interview. That's what this book is all about - getting ready to do your very best. While you are excited about getting a job, if you are like most people, you will be apprehensive about the job interview. Your ego is on the line. You might succeed, yet you might fail. The interviewer will ask you many questions to determine whether you are the right person for the job. To communicate that you are the best, you must let the prospective employer know your strengths and value. Yes, you believe they should hire you rather than other candidates. But how can you best manage the interview, so the interviewer shares this perception? What makes you so special in the eyes of the employer? Do you have something the others lack? Are you more capable, enthusiastic, or personable? Why should they think you are the best and hire you?

If the thoughts of being subjected to numerous questions, closely scrutinized by employers, and possibly rejected is enough to make your throat dry and your palms sweat, you are not alone. Most people are facing a prospective job interview experience with some nervous apprehension and fear. While they know the interview is a critical step in getting a job, they prefer avoiding it altogether because of its possible negative consequence - a rejection.

The job interview is a different type of job search activity from writing letters, using the telephone, or meeting people for information, advice, and referrals. Analogous in some ways to trying out for a part in a theatrical performance, the job interview places you on center stage for a part in the employer's organization. Employers want the best for their money. Your actions, both verbal and non-verbal, should communicate that you are the best one for the part.

Chapter 7: Know What You're Capable Of

Based on my experience, first, you must know below mentioned things about yourself:

What you're capable of?

1. Are you capable of doing a good work?

2. Do you have the capability to perform all the essential duties satisfactorily required for the position you are applying for?

3. Do you have ample potential in pursuance of carrying all the duties in every aspect in order to perform well?

Capability is one of the challenges of doing good work. If an employer decides you are incapable of doing your job they can dismiss you on the grounds of incapability. The capability issue usually arises when you are new to a job or something happens that start to affect your ability to do that job.

Poor performance and capability procedure

There are few basic points to bear in mind.

- It is up to your employer to decide what standard of performance it requires from its employees.

- Your employer has a right to insist that you perform well in all aspects of your role. The fact that you may be very good at one part but failing in another, may mean your employer is entitled to performance manage you.

- If your employer wants to or seeking to change the scope of your work or the standards expected from you, in most cases your employer should give you time and opportunity to adapt to the new expectations.

What is the purpose of the capability procedure?

- The purpose of it is to allow your employer to deal with any concern it may have about the performance of its employees.

Capability of meeting

If your employer has a capability procedure this will normally set out who is to conduct the capability meeting.

The purpose of the meeting should be to:

- Clarify the required standards and why your employer feels that you have not met them.

- Establish the likely reasons for your poor performance.

- Identity what can be done to assist you in improving your performance such as additional training or supervision?

- Set a timescale for review.

Following the meeting your employer should write to you confirming that was discussed at the meeting and informs you of the outcome.

What is a capability-based interview?

The most well-known method for directing meetings — however not by any means the only way — is utilizing the abilities. This depends on soliciting a set from inquiries, generally every inquiry managing one ability, that are intended to investigate the aptitudes you have and the confirmation that shows those abilities. The inquiries are more averse to investigate your specialized aptitude (however it does depend at work), since in many parts such abilities can be procured or created. Rather an ability based inquiry will, amongst different things, survey your capability to learn or create aptitude. It will investigate your behavioral qualities and the purported 'gentler abilities'; things like your capacity to impart well, how you fabricate affinity, or your qualities at impacting others. These qualities will be judged from the evidence and examples you present in your specific answers and also from your general performance and the way you conduct yourself during the interview.

A capability interview is therefore a way of giving you the opportunity to show how you demonstrate the key indicators. One of the most effective ways of doing that is by asking you to discuss examples of occasions where you have used and displayed the skills required. Presenting examples is a vital element of answering a question properly, but it is only one element. The next section describes in more detail the other elements of a good, persuasive answer.

Chapter 8: Types Of Interview Questions

All you have to do is convince your interviewer of your worthiness of the job as you will be asked different kinds of questions in the interview you attended. Here is a list of interview questions you might encounter on your way to securing your dream job:

1. Credential Verification Questions

These are also resume confirmation questions. These kinds of questions are usually asked to confirm the validity of the credentials presented in your resume. At this point, any right interview candidate should be able to answer these questions as you should have a sound knowledge of the content of your credentials. The questions asked here include:

• How long did you work at…………..?

• What Grade did you make?

2. Experience Verification Questions

These questions are asked to confirm your job experience, as stated in your resume. Job interview candidates are advised not to falsify expertise to be able to answer these questions correctly and function in your job position effectively. These questions include:

•What responsibilities did you perform in your previous job position?

•Were you relieved of your duties, or you resigned from your previous position and why?

3. Case Interview Questions

These questions are asked to know the ability of the candidate to solve a problem in a given situation. They usually concern the organization and how arising issues are handled.

4.Behavioral Interview Questions

These types of interview questions are more concentrated on the traditional kind of interview questions. And these types require you to respond with definite answers. Example is:

•I would like you to give me a particular pattern of how you did that?

5. Opinion Questions

These questions seek to know the point of view or opinion of an interview candidate about a particular scenario. These include questions like:

•When a situation like this arises, what will you do?

6. Competency-Based Interview Questions

These interview questions tend to examine the ability or competency of an interview candidate. They are usually asked to demonstrate a specific skill or attitude they claim to be good at. These include:

•Can you give an excellent demonstration of your marketing skills?

7. Brainteaser Questions

These questions usually test your knowledge of mathematics. Its either your mental ability to calculate in maths is questioned, or you are asked to prove your creative ability in formulating math's formulas.

As said earlier, the types of interview questions vary in different industries and companies. So, therefore, your preparation must be in all ramifications to increase the chances of getting your dream job.

Chapter 9: How To Handle Different Types Of Interviews And How To Be Successful In Each One

Whether you're in high school, university, recent college graduate, or out of the workplace, the job interview doesn't have to be an exhausting encounter. Interview is an opportunity for both you and the employer to decide whether or not you are fit.

Here is a step-by-step overview of a standard interview, including descriptions of what to expect throughout the process.

The Pre-Interview Stage

Before you go to the interview, you will have already taken a number of steps in the job application process; this is known as the pre-interview phase. During this period, you should have sent a cover letter, a resume, and any other necessary application materials to the hiring manager.

You might even have had a phone interview with the director before you were asked to an in-person interview. Therefore, before even heading into the meeting, the hiring manager learns a little more about your experience and your credentials.

You should feel confident—you are invited to have an interview because the manager thinks you could be a good company match!

The Interview Phase:

The Starting Your Interview may take place at your high school or college, but will generally take place at the company's office. Once you arrive, you may be asked (by a secretary or another employee) to wait until the hiring manager is ready to see you.

Most of the interviews are one-on - one interviews with the manager or supervisor with whom you would work most closely in the company. Occasionally, you will be meeting a human resources worker who is performing the company's hiring processes.

Problem Forms Interviews are likely to take place in the manager's office. She will begin with details regarding her work or the business or involve you in short discussions (questions about your experience, etc.), but most of the interview will be specific questions that will determine whether or not you will be suitable for the role.

Each interview will be precisely the same; each interviewer will pose slightly different questions. Nonetheless, most interviewers ask questions that assess both your overall actions and your abilities. Below are a few types of questions you might expect to come across; most interviewers will ask some of each type of question.

Verification Questions:

Such questions would ask you to provide objective information about yourself, such as your GPA, your specialty, the number of years you spent in your last work, etc. The interviewer may already know some of these responses and is therefore merely checking the facts of your resume.

Competence / Behavioral Questions:

The behavioral problem is one in which the interviewer asks you to explain a specific circumstance when you have shown a particular quality. Such queries show how you can cope with similar situations in a new job. An instance of a psychological problem is, "Describe the most difficult challenge you've encountered in your last career. How did you deal with it?" Contextual Questions:

The contextual query is one in which the respondent presents a hypothetical situation and the interviewee will clarify how she'd interact with it or how she'd treated it in the past. With this type of question, the interviewer wants to know how to deal with situations that may arise at the workplace. An instance of a contextual problem is, "What would you do if two members of your staff had a disagreement that compromised your productivity?"

Case Interview Questions:

If you apply for a management consulting or investment banking job, you would possibly just face a case interview question. In the case of interview questions, the employer gives the worker a company problem and advises the interviewee how to deal with the situation. Sometimes these are concerns regarding actual business conditions, but sometimes they are brain teasers that have no direct relevance to the work(' How many gas stations are there in Europe?'). Case interview questions enable interviewees to show their analytical skills and problem-solving skills.

Different Methods of Interviews:

Team Interviews While this article shows a typical interview with one hiring manager and one interviewee, there are other methods of interviews that you may find. Here are a few common examples.

Team Questions:

Another form of group interview you may find is an interview in which another recruitment director questions you and other candidates at the same time. In this case, you may be prompted by the investigator to answer the same questions, or to ask each of you different questions. Sometimes (especially if you're asked questions about a case interview), you're going to solve hypothetical problems as a team.

The form of group interview is one in which many interviewers ask you questions. Either the interviewers will form a panel and take turns asking you questions, or you will meet each other at a time.

Whether or not you are in a group interview, your interview questions are likely to remain a mix of verification, behavioral, and situational issues.

Interview Phase:

After Questions The interviewer can ask questions anytime from half an hour to an hour or more. After that, she'll probably ask you if you have any questions for her. This is your chance to ask questions about the organization and/or the place itself. This offers you another chance to sell yourself to the investigator, too. Again, the interview is your chance to see if the job is right for you, so feel comfortable asking questions.

After the "questions" process of the interview, the hiring manager will send you a tour of the workplace and even introduce you to other employees. A tour will give you the opportunity to see your new colleagues and evaluate the mood of the workplace.

While this is usually the end of the interview, certain interviews include additional components; for instance, you may be asked to give a speech to the hiring manager or to the personnel board. Nevertheless, if this is the case, you will have been informed about it in advance, and you will have had time to prepare.

At the end of the interview, don't ask the hiring manager to inform you whether or not you have a position. However, if she hasn't told you when you're coming back with an answer, feel free to ask her before you leave.

Post Interview Phase

The next phase of the job application process, the post-interview phase, will take place in the days following the interview. This is the time when the hiring manager (and anyone else involved in the hiring process) decides whether or not you are best suited to the position. This is also the time when you think about whether or not a job is best suited to you.

Many businesses will respond with a "yes" or a "no" within a week or two, although some organizations may take much longer to respond (especially if they conduct interviews over an extended period of time. However, some companies will not reply unless you are awaiting a job offer. If the organization then chooses between several candidates, you may even be asked to return for another try.

Chapter 10: Anticipating The Questions

First, you have to ask yourself: "What questions commonly appear in interviews?"

The interview process is a mechanism by which employers get to know their prospects. They ask for information that are not written on your CVs so that they will know what to expect and what not to expect from you. The process is two-way. In the interview, it is not only the employer that should do the assessment. You, the applicant, should also get the feel of the work atmosphere.

Many applicants fail big time because they do not get to anticipate the interview questions that are thrown at them. Surprised, they are caught off guard and the next tendency is to panic. When panic strikes, the entire interview is anticipated to be a great mess. To avoid this scenario, just read this chapter and prepare for the questions.

Here are some of the questions that are likely to be covered:

academic achievements and diplomas or certifications earned

work background experiences

interpersonal skills like leadership capability

personal and professional goals

personal and professional skills

career objectives

how well you understand the role

personal strengths

personal weaknesses

Other forms of questions are the following:

What decisions led to your choice of academic institution?

What are the most challenging parts of your previous job?

In what particular scenario were you able to show your effectiveness as a team player?

What are your reasons for leaving your previous job?

Give a five-year plan in terms of how you will develop your career.

What skills and capabilities are you most proud of?

How can you be of use to the company?

What is your biggest achievement in life?

That challenges do you anticipate in this particular job that you are applying for?

Never assume that the interviewer has done his homework – most interviewers do not read the CVs at all. So you need to supply as much information as possible so that you will create the right impression. The responses should be packaged in such a way that your interviewer has no clue of who you are, how much you have achieved, and where you intend to lead your life.

If you find challenging questions in the interview, there are options that are ready for you. Such questions are usually given to determine if you can act appropriately despite the pressure. Here are some tips:

Prepare well for questions that you can anticipate

Admit your limitation or lack of knowledge – it is much better that waffling or lying

When your opinion is asked, do not be too radical or too conservative

To illustrate your point, try your best to provide examples

Never assume that your interviewer has an "expected set of answers"

If things get a bit too personal, remember that you can respectfully decline answering the interviewer's question. You can do this if you think that the question is not at all connected to your application for the job.

On the other hand, if it will affect your manner of fulfillment of the role, provide an appropriate response. Do not give out unnecessary information especially if it will jeopardize your safety and privacy.

There are instances, however, when the interview is done in groups. You should be prepared for such a scenario so that you will stand out and be more than just a face in the crowd. What should be expected in group interviews?

Discussions with other candidates wherein the facilitator and interviewer will ask them to complete a certain task or discuss a certain topic

A common question for everyone and the candidates will take turn answering

Group interviews are commonly done by companies that believe in the importance of group interactions. Such kinds of interviews are opportunities to manifest your strengths. The following are usually expected from the candidates:

To be able to show that they have sufficient working knowledge of the given topic

To demonstrate the capability to take turns, listen to other people's points of view, and understand their points accordingly

To show that you have the capacity to act as a leader and give a point of convergence for a diverse group of applicants

To do positive intervention if there are dominant group members

To summarize the activity or build consensus among different group members

Remember, there are principles that you have to remember in group interviews. First, learn to elaborate. You need to know how to supply relevant illustrations and useful examples. In addition, you have to know how to come up with feasible alternatives. A good team player would know another approach in reaching a desired end. Next, summarization is a desired skill. Remember to include even the points you do not agree with. Lastly, a good team player is an inclusive person. One should be "others" oriented.

Given the chance to ask a question to the one who interviews you, you should have two to three in mind. Here are the most intelligent ones:

What sort of professional and personal trainings may be expected from the company?

What expansion plans do the organization intend to engage in the future?

If ever lucky enough to be accepted, when should I start reporting for duty?

Having these questions in mind and preparing questions show your level of eagerness and genuine passion to take on the role offered by the company.

Chapter 11: Common Questions And Answers

Many people say that your first job interview is a lot like your first date. It's filled with pressure and courtship. Aside from presenting ourselves correctly, the real tension comes from the questions that will be asked and how you respond with answers as impressive as your physical presence. Although, no person can foretell the exact questions that will be asked in your first interview, there are common questions that interviewers find effective in determining who's the right fit for the job. We do not encourage canned answers for every question, instead this is very helpful to serve as a guide.

Tell me about yourself.

This is the simplest yet the most vital question an interviewer can ask. You're the best person to know everything about yourself, and yet, many fail to nail it. When you are asked to talk about yourself, it doesn't mean that you let the interviewer know about your whole story. The key is to keep it short and simple. One to two minutes is enough. Although the topic is about you, do not get too casual. Remember that you are still in an interview. Pace yourself, make sure that your body catches up with your brain before you speak and show some body language or positions that tell him you are comfortable and excited to answer his question about yourself. You should not include the information which are already written in your resume. The simplest way to start is with an easy topic like what you are doing or your career focus. Next, you can transition to your professional accomplishments. You can use some data results of your hard work or you can simply choose one to two milestones of your career. To sum it up, talk about how these experiences inspired you to look for challenges and opportunities.

How did you find out about the position?

Let's say you hear the job position from a friend who is already working in the company, give the name and tell the interviewer why you are excited to be a part of it as well. If you read the job post in an article or in a magazine, share what about the company caught your attention. Even if you found the job post on a job listing website, highlight why you decided to apply to that company among all the companies listed.

Why should we hire you?

Here goes the intimidating question. It sounds difficult, but this question actually opens a perfect stage for you to sell yourself. Not all of the interviewees are asked this question because most of the time, it is asked if many candidates are qualified for the job. Show that you're more than just qualified and that it is the best choice to pick you. Remember, the hiring manager also risks his reputation in recommending an applicant and it is understandable that he is looking for a relief as early as the interview process.

The best way to start is to reiterate your strengths. Make sure it compliments the top requirements in the job description. It may include experience, trainings, key accomplishments and awards or recognition. You can also use success stories in certain projects and of course, highlight your skills that made it work. Again, the trick is to be brief but concise. You don't want to reiterate all of the awards and recognition you listed on your resume but you just have to pick what most likely will set you apart from other candidates. If you already discussed some of it in the earlier course of the interview, you can just come up with a broader summary of those pieces and emphasize it with a right dose of confidence. It is helpful to review the important qualifications before going to the interview to help you prepare and get ready to answer this question.

What are your fears / weaknesses?

Now that you know how to handle the 'What are your strengths?' kind of question, you should take the 'What are your weaknesses?' question with a little more care. The trick here is balance. You don't want an absolute negative answer like ' I tend to put off projects sometimes, causing me to miss deadlines ', but we also don't want something like ' I don't think I have weaknesses'. The reason why you are being asked this question is not to reveal your weak spots but to measure your self-awareness. Of course, no one's perfect so the interviewer wants to know how you deal with your own challenges. Start off by stating your shortcoming but do not use words that sound as bad as **paranoid** or **alcoholic**. Choose the word that sounds more professional and appropriate and phrase it in a positive light. Example, " I am a perfectionist. Sometimes, I look into details too much, making sure everything is right the first time." Then, transition to following up the weakness you mention by telling him what you are doing to overcome that weakness. If you can properly describe the steps you've taken to get away with this shortcoming, you will appear strong and in charge of your own development. If from the start of the interview you are already not sure if you are fit for the position, use your lack of experience or unmatched requirements as a shortcoming and turn it around to emphasize your strengths.

How do you see yourself in five years?

The interviewer is curious about your personal future plans and that is why you're being asked this question. He wants to see your honesty and if you're capable of setting realistic goals. Aligned with it is the role of the company to you. The hiring manager wants to hear your expectations for your position, if you are looking forward to having career growth, if you have an ambition, and if you want to fulfill that ambition with that company. The key is to be realistic about where the position can take you. If you feel like that position is just a stepping-stone to what you really wanted, you can say that you're not quite sure what the future holds but the experience in that position will definitely be a factor to what your decisions may be.

Why did you leave your current job? Or Why were you let go?

This question makes you swipe your hanky to your forehead. The challenge with this question is your ability to maintain your self-esteem and not be affected with your emotions. Again, the key is honesty. Not too honest that you would depreciate yourself and play as a poor employee, but just enough honesty to precisely state what happened. Here, **'less is more'** applies. Speak without hesitation because if you stutter or over-explain, you will sound as if you are covering up something. Before you set foot in this interview, make sure that you already came to terms with whatever emotion you had from being let go. If you're successful in leaving your feelings behind, you'll be able to speak genuinely about your mistakes with your focus intact. Remember, you are talking to a human and they make mistakes too. All of us have our own fair share of these experiences so what's more important is the ability to learn from it. Discuss what you learned and don't doubt yourself. They all want that confident person to walk through their door. Finally, never ever badmouth your previous company or employer.

Do you have a question?

A job interview is not a one-way road. Of course, you already expected that you will be the one answering the questions, but not necessarily, all of it. Interview is also meant for you to gauge if that position is right for you. It is equally important that you ask basic information you feel you need to know in case you get hired. In some cases, this is also the interviewee's way of saying 'are you listening?' Here are some of the questions that are okay to ask:

-What will be the day-to-day tasks in this position?

-Is there any immediate projects that need to be taken care of?

- What attributes do I need to have to succeed in this position?

- What are the possible challenges that I may face in this position?

- Were you expecting a change in responsibility in this position over the next year or two?

- How will the training be?

- Is there an opportunity for career growth?

- What are the key things that I need to accomplish in the first three months?

- How will I be evaluated?

- What is your favorite part about working here?

- What are the current goals of the company and how can I help to achieve it?

- Who will I work with the most?

- To whom will I directly report to?

-Is there any other information I can provide that will be helpful?

Just like your first date, the best way to a successful interview is to be yourself. After all, only you would know if you will get a call back.

Chapter 12: Tell Me Something About Yourself

When a potential employer is asking this questions they are wanting to look more into your work life and not necessarily your personal life, however this does not mean you are not allowed to talk about your personal life, so long as it pertains and compliments your professional appeal. Generally, the employer is searching for aspects of yourself which tie you to the company values and of course your work ethic. Do you participate in behaviors which are risky when applying for a position which would be someone who is not quickly replaceable?

Employers are not allowed to discriminate within the employment process, however if you are openly admitting that you like to disappear without warning for weeks on end, this would be a strong deterrent for any employer. When asked this question it is best to begin with the job you currently have or your last position and work your way backwards until you reach your education and any certifications you may have.

If you volunteer in your free time or are working towards higher education within the field you are applying which would be beneficial to the company down the road, it would be wise to provide that information as well. Do you do any activities in your spare time which could help your job? If so those activities would also be worth mentioning. Any information about yourself which shows you would be an asset to the company because of your continued pursuit to be better in the position for which you are seeking employment.

A great way to answer this question is by using positive adjectives to describe yourself. Add in your years of experience and your skills which make you a good fit for the position and the company. Talk about how you are a person who is looking to expand on certain goals and skills and explain how the position you are applying for would be a great fit for those goals. Finish out by talking about your own desire to learn, grow, and contribute to the mission of the company.

With this question it is important to avoid any hot button topics which could raise a debate such as religion and politics. You may mention you have a family if you do or leisurely activities but do avoid speaking of anything which may raise an eyebrow or concern that you may be untrustworthy or potentially unreliable. This does not mean you should avoid telling your potential employer who you are but rather this is a suggestion to do your best to keep your conversation to the job and alluding to what potential you have to give more to the company than any other candidate they will see.

Be honest with your credentials and do not spend your time elaborating on your resume. This will come later in the interview when they begin to ask you specific questions pertaining to the position at hand. Avoid at all costs bragging about your successes and keep your response friendly but to the point.

When speaking about past positions avoid leaving out jobs which could have been found through their research or are mentioned on your resume. Doing so will cause the employer to then focus specifically on that which you were trying to avoid. If you are wishing to avoid speaking about a specific job it is best to still mention it and behave as though the position wasn't an issue. Talk freely and honestly without being negative towards the position, company or employees.

WHY YOU?

This question may seem like a throw away in an interview but in reality the employer is looking for a response which shows you truly feel a connection to the position and feel you are a good fit. If your response is wavering or seems as though you are uncertain of yourself, they may feel as though you are not the best fit.

Qualifications are only a portion of why a person is hired for a position and sometimes it can come down to how well you sell yourself through confidence.

When asked this question it is best to focus on your skill set. What kinds of skills and talents can you bring to the table which will really shine? Rather than focusing on why you want the job, perhaps because it is your first real position, or you really need it for financial reasons, focus on the reason you want the job as being a good fit with your talents.

Focusing also on your experience as a reason why you should be chosen will help you in selling yourself to your interviewer. Without becoming a broken record you can always keep the answer simple by stating politely something along the lines of, "As you can see from my resume, I have extensive experience in this type of position." This response gives you an answer that does not warrant repeating your entire resume or answers already provided from other responses.

As well as referring to skills and previous experience you can talk about your personal passion for the work the position provides. Having a personal passion for something work related is always a desired quality by employers because this means the employee will work harder and be more invested in their job than someone who is only there for a paycheck. Those who have personal passion tend to last longer in jobs and are willing to put in more time and effort for the betterment of the company.

With this question avoid talking about how much money you would like to make. Now is the time to sell yourself not to discuss the subject of money. More often than not employers will not ask questions regarding salary if they are not considering you for a position. Do not rush out of the gate in your interview discussing money, even though the topic is important, as this will imply that you are only applying for the position for the money and not because you are really interested in the company or the job itself.

Chapter 13: Preparing For A Job Hunt

Before embarking on a job hunt, it is useful to understand your reasons for wanting or needing a new job. Your needs and desires will direct your efforts, from the amount of time you devote to which avenues you pursue, and help you to shape your goals for the future. As the old saying goes, it is easier to hit a target you can see. Having a firm idea of what you are looking for in the job market will help ensure that you do not end up in a position you are unqualified, or that makes you miserable.

Depending on your situation, you might fall into one of three categories. High Priority, those who need a job immediately; Medium Priority, those who are ready for a new job but aren't in a major rush; and Low Priority, those who desire a new job but can afford to take their time. While members of each category should affix a clear goal in their minds before sending resumes or searching job boards, the scope of the goal and amount of time allotted for hitting it will change. To determine which category you fall into, you can consider which of the following situations is closest to yours:

High Priority

You are unemployed

Unemployment can happen to anyone, regardless of education level or status. For those who have money saved or other revenue streams, not having a job is not necessarily a tragic event. Those who require a steady paycheck, however, probably need to find a position quickly.

Your job is in jeopardy

Signs that your job may be in trouble include a breakdown in communication between yourself and your boss (e.g., moving from speaking to emailing); lack of concern on your boss's part about your job fulfillment; or significant financial troubles in your department or the entire company.

You are about to graduate from college

The next step after graduation is finding a job, but many students are under extra pressure to do so; according to 2013 data from the Consumer Financial Protection Bureau, one in five American households have student loans, which equates to over $1.1 trillion in outstanding student loan debt.

Medium Priority

You are not experiencing growth or are unhappy at your current company

Everyone has bad days at work, but if you find that your work is unchallenging or you dread going in each day, you might be ready for a move. Perhaps your boss does not allow you to take on new tasks or everyone you work with is negative. However, because your job is secure, you are not rushed to find a new one.

Your salary is low relative to the Industry-Standard

If your peers at your company or in your industry are paid more or if your boss has consistently put off giving you a raise, you might be considering moving to a company that will offer you better compensation for your skills. Unsure as to whether you are being compensated properly? Visit the U.S. Bureau of Labor Statistics' website (bls.gov) and search the Occupational Outlook Handbook, which lists median pay for most jobs and positions. Caution is the watchword in this situation, though — you may not want to give up a good job if you only have a vague idea that something out there might be better.

Low Priority

You are ready for a change of career

Whether you've decided that your current career is not for you or you are simply ready to explore a new field, switching careers often takes time and patience. You might need additional education or training, which means you may need to stick it out in your current place for a while longer. If you are lucky enough already to have a steady career or job, you can most likely take your time while you pursue your new dream.

Your job is stable, but you do not see any chance of promotion

Granted, promotions are not guaranteed in any company, but if you've been consistently skipped over or your company only hires from the outside, you might find your efforts better rewarded in a different company. This is especially important for those who are ambitious or already have a system of goals in place. Job seekers in this position, as with those who are looking for a higher salary, would do well to be prudent — like the cliché says, a bird in the hand is worth two in the bush.

Once you've determined whether you are a High, Medium or Low Priority job seeker by identifying your main reason for finding a new job, you are ready to perform three simple tasks that will put you on the road to job hunting success.

Number 1:

Identify your time commitment. Members of the High Priority category might need to devote several hours per day, while those in the Low Priority category might only set aside an hour or two per week. Either way, consider how much time you realistically have (don't forget to take into account family obligations, etc.), decide what your time commitment is, and stick to it. Some days it will be difficult, but you'll have a greater chance of being successful in the end through sheer consistency.

Number 2:

Identify, in writing, your job goal. Record the title of the position you'd like to hold (even if it is the same as your current position). Write out a job description, including what you'll be responsible for, the departments or people who will answer to you, the tasks you'll perform, and how you'll help the company by performing your job. You can type this or write it on a notecard, but keep it handy. As you begin to choose jobs to apply for and undergo interviews, you'll be able to compare what's being offered with what you truly want.

Number 3:

Research your job goal. Setting an unrealistic goal is setting yourself up for failure, so take an honest look at where you are in your career, the skills you have, and where you'd like to be, and then look for any shortcomings you need to address. If, for example, those in your profession who're being promoted have a certification you do not have, you may need to take a step back from the job search to elevate your skills and credentials. For a list of websites that will help you find more information about your field and its requirements, you can visit the Resources section at the end of this book

After you've spent time taking an in-depth look at why you are searching for a new job and what your goal for the future is, you are ready to begin the process of creating a resume, finding jobs to apply for, and interviewing.

Chapter 14: Questions To Help You Find Your Dream Career

It can be very difficult in trying to decide what your dream career is. For many of us we get so caught up in trying to do the job we have we don't have much time left to spend thinking about our dream career. You have to decide whether you want to make a complete career change from the one you are presently doing or do you just want to make some minor shifts within the one you are presently in. By asking yourself a few simple questions it can make planning your dream career much easier. Below is a list of questions to ask yourself in regards to choosing a career path.

1) If I could change careers with a friend who would that be? _____ Because?

2) I have always been interested in _____ it interests me because_____

3) If I had the proper education I would want to be_____ because_____

4) If I went back to school I would take_____
because_____

5) My friends and co-workers say that I am really great at _____because_____
_____

6) What I really like about my current job is_____because_____
_____

7) I would like to do more _____ if my boss would let me because_____

8) If I had to work on a Saturday I would choose_____

because_____

9) I want to be known for _____

because_____

Once you have answered these questions take a closer look at your answers. Do you see any patterns with your answers? You may see some common themes such as you may be interested in caring for others for example. These questions are not going to point out a specific career choice for you but they will help you to understand what you value and enjoy. Knowing what you want to be known for is a great way to get started towards improving your skills to get that dream job that you want.

Get Career Insight Through Journaling.

Below are a few methods or techniques that you can try in getting started with a journal.

1) **Brain Drain.** This particular technique was popularized with Julia Cameron in her book "The Artist's Way" when she suggests that you write down what is on your mind when you first wake up in the morning. This is writing stream-of-consciousness long hand. This exercise will help you to confront, provoke, clarify, and prioritize the day at hand. Try this method and see what type of results you get.

2) **Using a Prompt.** Having questions is a great way to help in getting your writing started. For example to help you to think a little deeper about your dream career a good prompt might be: What am I afraid of? Everyday for a week write this question and your answer to it. Think about your job, goal, and your career. What are you afraid of? Are you afraid of failing? Maybe your fear is of being found out to be a fraud. By putting these

thoughts in your work journal you can help to gain clarity about what is holding you back from success or limiting your success. You may find that writing about the things that you fear will help to free you from the hold that they have on you.

3) **Make a List.** Make a list of deep thoughts regarding your career.

• Make a list of your achievements that you have accomplished in your career. Try and focus on the things that you have done not on things that you have yet to accomplish

• Create a list for your ideal future, what would your future be like if you had your dream job or career? Think of what would be involved in a perfect day at your dream job

4) **Things I Used to Believe.** Make a list of of things that you used to believe regarding your career. Perhaps you at one time believed you would never be able to confront your boss who was treating you unfairly. By seeing how your beliefs

changed over time can help to create a positive reflection point. What better way to capture your personal development stories with your career than in a journal? If you are in a hurry just write three positive things that happened that day.

If writing a journal is something you have never tried before as a career tool now would be a great time to start one. By using a journal as a career tool it will help you to search throughout your professional career. So what are you waiting for get writing!

Chapter 15: We Will Call You

Once the interview is completed and you are on the way out or even a bit before that while the interview questions are being finalized the interviewer will announce to you when you should be expecting to hear from them. All the professional companies will announce a time window that you should expect their final answer either that is positive or negative. Usually a normal waiting period will be a week.

At no point you should contact the company from your side and ask them what is the status or feedback of your job interview. Do not be impatient. If the days pass by and you do not receive a call or an email from the company notifying about the results then is likely that you did not get the job.

If you do receive a phone call within the time frame mentioned you should be again as professional as possible. If the company advises that you have successfully passed the interview and you are hired stay concentrated in order to gain information on when exactly you should start and if further action is required from your side such as bring some documentation or certificates on the first day of work.

On the other hand if the company is calling to let you know that there is someone else selected for the job once again you should be as professional and polite as possible. Try to show your gratitude for the chance provided to participate on the job interview process. If you are really professional on the rejection call rather than be aggressive and not polite, then the HR will have you on the top list for possible new openings in the near future and this happens really often.

A frequent scenario that also occurs within the business world is that a company hired someone else for the job you have applied for and the HR manager called you to notify about the results. Now only few days after the new employee started at the job position and for a variety of reasons he has quit the job and left. Then if you have been one the candidates that was really professional and polite when you have received the rejection call you will be the first to get a call and been notified that although you have been rejected few days back they will like to proceed with you for the company current job position and you can start on this coming Monday or the 1st of the next month.

A lot of people which am sharing this with them they do not believe that something like that is likely to ever happen but you will be surprised how often something like that occurs.

Another frequent scenario which occurs in the business world is that HR Managers, CEOs and CFOs of the same field companies usually know each other and they keep professional relationships. Now for some reason the company you have applied and interviewed for decided that they will proceed with another candidate for the job because that candidate has more experience on the field but you as a person managed to create an excellent impression then its very likely that they will recommend you to another HR Manager that they know that they are also looking for someone with your qualifications.

Chapter 16: Managing Third-Party Recruiters

If you have not applied for jobs in a while, or if you are relatively new to the job market, then you need to pay close attention to this chapter.

Who Are Third-Party Recruiters?

Third-party recruiters (also known as headhunters, external recruiters, staffing or talent acquisition specialists, talent agents, among other titles) are professionals who companies hire to help them find candidates for open positions. The recruiters can either work for small or larger organizations or they can be independent contractors.

Regardless of where they work, it is important to understand that third-party recruiters work for the companies they are helping, not you. They have a financial interest in placing you, therefore, all of their advice to you must be taken with this in mind.

Well, one of the work-arounds for companies (other than ATS) is to have these external recruiters take care of this part of the process for them, so they don't have to comb through piles of résumés. Recruiters will do the initial screening of candidates and then present companies with several options, so the process is more manageable and efficient.

There are both positives and negatives with having third-party recruiters as part of your job search. Let's discuss both.

The Positives

1. If you connect with a recruiter and he or she winds up sending your résumé to a company, then you are substantially increasing your chances of your résumé being seen and then getting called for an interview.

2. A lot of times these recruiters have established relationships with the

companies they represent which also means they have a good idea of what a particular hiring manager is looking for and what types of questions you can expect during the interview. This is incredibly valuable information.

3. Recruiters will help negotiate your salary and other benefits on your behalf so you do not need to speak with the company directly about any of those topics.

4. If you do not get an interview or an offer, and you enjoyed working with the recruiter, then you now have a new contact for possible future opportunities.

The Negatives

1. Recruiters only get paid (or earn a decent portion of their compensation) when you agree to a company's offer. In other words, they work on commission. Therefore, they may try to justify a weak dollar offer or a company's unwillingness to give you an extra week of vacation in the hopes that you'll sign your offer letter

so they can get paid. Only **you** know what's really best for you.

2. Low barrier to entry. In today's world, almost anyone can be a recruiter and the market is, therefore, saturated with them. It can be a very cut-throat business when there are so many players which is why it's important to understand the potential pitfalls.

3. Some recruiters will use under-handed tactics to try and extract information from you that they can potentially use for their own purposes. More on this in a minute.

Over the years, I have heard (and personally experienced) many stories about questionable, rude, and/or unethical behavior toward job seekers by external recruiters. Recruiters who behave in this way are not worth your time. Only spend time working with the true professionals.

How to Connect with Recruiters

You can connect with recruiters in two ways: they reach out to you (usually via LinkedIn or your email) or you actively seek them out. Let's take each scenario separately.

They Reach out to You

This is common especially when your LinkedIn profile is updated. They are looking for potential candidates who may be willing to entertain the idea of switching companies.

If you are contacted by a recruiter, first make sure they want to discuss a specific position and you get the job description from them in writing before sending your résumé along. The reason this is important is because there are some recruiters out there who will "fish" for professionals to add into their databases and will lie about having an open position just to get your résumé and other details.

Story: Here is an actual email exchange to illustrate what I mean:

A recruiter sent an email with a brief, generic job description for a position in a job seeker's general geographic location. The company and location were not revealed.

Job Seeker: Thank you for the email. Can you tell me who the company is and the location?

No response from the recruiter. Job Seeker follows up with another email three days later.

Recruiter: This is a semi-confidential search in that we are disclosing the company once we have had a pre-qualification discussion via phone.

Job Seeker: I understand. I'd like to learn more. When is a good time to chat?

Recruiter: Are you actively looking?

Job Seeker: I'm keeping my options open. I'm free Thursday morning. Will that work?

No response from the recruiter.

No decent recruiter is going to drag his feet when there is an interested candidate for an open position. This exchange was highly suspect from the radio silence the recruiter gave the job seeker after **the recruiter** initially reached out. Fortunately for the job seeker, no real time was wasted and the recruiter only got the fact that the job seeker was interested. It doesn't matter because that recruiter has already proven not to be worth the job seeker's time.

Look out for nonsense like this.

There are right ways to build relationships and there are many wrong ways to go about it. Just be diligent and aware like you would when someone you don't know reaches out and starts asking for sensitive information.

You Reach out to Them

If you find you are having trouble searching on your own, either because of time or other constraints, then you can proactively reach out to recruiters as they may be able to help you.

There are also independent recruiters who are easily found on LinkedIn.

If they're smart, they will take your call and if they're professional, they'll be honest with you regarding whether they can ultimately help you then or in the future. In these cases, you will send them your résumé so they can get a clear understanding of your background and what you're looking to do next.

Note: In either case, never hand over your résumé unless you first have their agreement, in writing, that they will not send your résumé to any company without your written permission. Any good recruiter will understand this.

What's the big deal if they send out my résumé? It can't hurt, right?

Wrong.

The reason this clarification is necessary is because there are some recruiters who will send your résumé to companies without you even knowing! The problem with this is the company receiving your résumé does not know that you did not give consent, and then **you** can potentially look bad (without you even knowing), especially if a recruiter is over the line or aggressive with the company.

Don't let someone else tarnish your reputation with unprofessionalism. Guard your résumé closely and only give it out directly to companies or recruiters whom you trust and/or are comfortable with.

Speaking with Recruiters

Once recruiters have your résumé, you will most likely have a call with them so they can learn a little more about you and what you're looking to do next. This is very common and should be an easy conversation. The initial phone call should be casual but professional and fairly brief. You should not be surprised by any questions or made to feel uncomfortable in any way.

Be cognizant of how the conversation is going. A good recruiter will want to know your work history, where you are looking to go next in your career, how far you would be willing to commute, and possibly what your salary requirements would be.

Questions to Watch out for

Unfortunately, this is not always the case. All of the below questions (among others), including the many variations, are red flags. All of these questions are meant to work against you as negotiating leverage for a company; or are just plain nosy and rude.

Do not answer any of these and, if more than one comes up during a conversation, don't continue to engage with this particular recruiter. They are not worth your time.

Note: The same goes for company employees. They should **not** be asking you these types of questions either.

- What is your current salary?

- What is your salary history?

- What is the lowest salary that you'll accept?

- Do you have a family/kids?

- Do you own a home?

- How old are you?

- What year did you graduate college?

- Where are you from originally?

While some of these questions may come across as a recruiter innocently wanting to get to know you better, the fact is that **all** of these questions are offensive and none of his business.

If you reached out to a recruiter, then you will discuss what you are looking to do next as well as whether there are any current openings that might be a potential fit. And, if you are speaking to him about a specific role, then you will talk about your work history, your salary requirements, and also work to learn as much about the new role as he can tell you. That's it.

All of those other questions are totally irrelevant and, in some cases, illegal.

Recruiters are not your career counselor, friend, or mentor. They are agents for a company and are trying to earn a commission by placing you. Your relationship with a recruiter is also a business relationship. You don't need to answer offensive questions to be seriously considered for open positions, so don't allow them to make you feel small in any way. You are in total control of these interactions.

Finally, like with many of the topics in this book, use your gut. If recruiters (or anyone else you connect with) are making any types of disparaging or negative comments about you or your work history, you don't have to tolerate it. Your work history is what it is and you have nothing to apologize for. Don't get involved with someone who doesn't take the time to understand who you are and what you are looking to do next. Do not get drawn into a bad relationship. If it doesn't feel right, walk away and cut off all communication. There are plenty of good recruiters out there with whom you can work.

Knowledge Is Power

This book, especially this chapter, is meant to empower you on your journey to your next job. The more information you have about all of these moving parts, the more powerful you will be which will quickly translate into confidence.

Confidence impacts everything we do and everyone we meet in a positive way. Having confidence in yourself is the keystone to becoming a strong and successful job seeker, and this confidence will serve you best during the most important part of the process, the interview.

Chapter 17: Getting To The Introductions

Introductions are a great way to set the right tone of an interview. You say something awkward, and the rest of the interview will follow suit. You say something informal, the interviewer fidgets a little, and there goes your confidence. Remain too unapproachable and stiff, and the interviewer would likely close down too and will compromise the comfort level on both ends. Introductions need to be friendly and professional. Here's how to get them right.

Introduce Yourself

The chances are you will be seated in an empty room, and the interviewers will then enter. While you wait, you can take out your pen and paper and place them in front of you. Sip some water and take a few deep breaths. Avoid the urge to probe around the table or room or check your phone 'one last time' before the interview begins.

Once the interviewers enter, get up to greet them and give them those now perfected handshake and smiles. Ask them how their day has been. In case the interviewers are already sitting in the room. Walk right up to them with a steady, confident walk, move your hand forward to initiate a handshake and introduce yourself. Do not seat yourself until asked to. Some interviewers like to take the lead and will ask you to introduce yourself. If they remain silent, take the lead and start the introduction yourself. Your introduction needs to be concise and focused on why you are actually there. You should work on your introduction like a sales pitch. Begin with providing details about yourself, who you are, where you are from, what have you studied and where from. Then move on to your professional skills and experiences and finish off by talking about your overall career goals briefly. Talking about your career goals enables the interviewer to assess how your goals fit in with those of the company and whether they would be assistive towards each other. Your introduction should be no more than five sentences and should be customized according to your company's research. Revise it again and again. Does it do justice to all your skills and experiences? Is your introduction of who you truly are as a professional? Would you hire you based on this introduction? The introduction should be able to make a lasting impact all on its own. But avoid a 10-page long essay on how you started your journey as a little boy with big dreams. The interviewers aren't interested.

It makes sense to practice it in front of the mirror beforehand so that you can state it with conviction and confidence. Here is a sample introduction for your perusal:

This is short and concise and enables the interviewer to get a better understanding of your skills, experience, and future plans.

It also serves as an icebreaker to more complex and targeted questions.

Don't Use Slang Language

They say it takes the first ten steps, first 10 seconds and the first ten words to make a lasting impression. So far, you have aced the steps and the seconds, don't let the words destroy your chances of a great career prospect. There is a lot of debate over whether you should use formal or informal language. Using your entire vocabulary during a single interview could make you boring and uninteresting while using an informal language could make you like an unprofessional. Either way, one thing to keep in mind is to understand the relationship between the interviewer and yourself and converse accordingly. Many times, fresh graduates especially, ripe with confidence and drive to finally put all their knowledge to profitable use, end up speaking to their interviewers like they would with their mentors, teachers, and mates. Mentors and teachers want that informal relationship with their students so that they can make themselves feel accessible. Interviewers, on the other hand, are still in the assessment process, they are trying to understand whether you are professional enough to deal with clients, customers, co-workers, and management heads. Avoid using words like 'you guys' and 'hell yes' with the interviewer. Instead, opt for words like 'the company' and 'of course.' The kind of tone and language that you use will depend a lot on the environment and your interviewer. The good idea is to mirror the language your interviewer uses and allow him to set the tone. But there are certain words and phrases that have more impact while others that can be fatal to your chances of a successful interview. Following is everything you need to know:

Words that Have an Impact

Opt for powerful and positive words during the interview. Make a list of all the words the company often uses to define their goals, values, and culture and incorporate them as much as possible.

Adding those words in your own sentence structures would automatically form a link between the company and yourself and the interviewer is bound to get infected by your charm and motivation to work in the company.

The choice of words used to convey the same message could be delivered in very different ways. For instance, here are two examples of the same message: 'I helped the team with their projects' and 'I provided solutions to make the projects successful for my team.' Both of these sentences are trying to convey leadership roles. However, where the former sentence is vague and doesn't define your role in the projects, the second one specifically states how your role in the team was an important one to make campaigns and projects successful. Certain words and phrases just have more impact compared to other generic terms. Following is a list of some of the most powerful words to use during your interview:

Decision Maker

This is the Don Corleone to job interview words. It has such power and authority. Using this word instantly puts you in an impactful position. It showcases that you are not only confident about your skills but know how to use them to lead the team forward aptly.

Passion

Interviewers want to know whether you'd come to clock your hours or serve as an integral component in the company's growth. Passion shows that you are the later. But don't just be a 'passionate person.' Know what you are passionate about and communicate the same. You could be passionate about progress, leadership, teamwork, project management, growth, etc. Other similar words are enthusiastic, energized, motivated, love, interested, etc.

Responsibility

This is a word that takes ownership of your actions. Do you care about the bigger picture? Are you willing to take up the responsibility assigned to you and treat it as an integral part of your being? Will you meet and exceed the established standards of work? This powerful word portrays all these in affirmations. Other similar words are coordination, effectiveness, detail-oriented, deadlines and efficiency.

Management and Leadership

You don't necessarily need to use these words only if you are applying for leadership roles. These words have an impact no matter what position you are applying for. Both these words acknowledge teamwork and the ability to be a part of it in an assertive and respectful manner. Other similar words are teamwork, build, accomplish, accelerate, deliver, innovate, negotiate, developed, etc.

Achieved

This word alone enables you to take ownership of your successes. The word in itself makes you sound like a winner in the role that you are applying for. But don't just go you are an achiever, follow it with something constructive that you have indeed recently achieved. Other similar words include presented, influenced, persuaded, approved, etc.

Recommend and Suggest

These are great ways to offer ideas and talk about ideas that got results delivered. These words, like decision-maker, suggest that you know how to take up responsibility and come up with quality ideas to achieve your milestones and tasks. They also suggest that you aren't easily run down by other more assertive employees and know how to hold your ground with your opinions and suggestions.

Collaborate

No matter what job or position you are applying for, there is a great chance that you wouldn't be working in isolation; and the interviewer would want to know if you are a people's person and flexible enough to respect and encourage other people's views. This word suggests that respect other people's opinions and knows how to work as a team for the sake of the bigger picture. Other similar words include teamwork, partnership, assistance, unity, etc.

Industry Specific Buzzwords

Every industry has jargon and buzzwords that they like to throw around for a sense of belonging. You are probably already aware of these words if you have been working in the industry for long enough. If not, then read up to familiarize yourself with it. You will hardly find this in textbooks. Read books written by people in your industry, follow them on LinkedIn and Twitter, and check relevant videos and blogs.

Words that Could Kill

Just like positive words can leave a positive impact, negative words too will leave a lasting unfavorable impression. Following are some words you need to eliminate from your dictionary, at least for the time being:

No

This two letter word has such a negative impact that you might not be able to recover from it. Avoid answering questions with a simple 'yes' or 'no' anyway. But even if you need to disagree, make a smarter selection of words. If the interviewer says, 'Will you reassign work given to you to other employees?' Rather than just a blunt 'no,' opt for something like 'I am a responsible person and would prefer always completing the tasks assigned to me myself.' The latter has just so much positivity and emphasis on values and gives you an opportunity to reflect them. Words similar to 'no' include never, will not, not really, negative, etc.

Whatever

This is such a buzz kill. It shows a lack of interest, lack of innovation, lack of anything, and everything really. If you don't want the interviewer to treat your application like a 'whatever' don't 'whatever' anything!

You Know

Many times, candidate use this word generously to form a connection with the interviewer; to let the interviewer know that both of you are on the same page. But the interviewer doesn't want to form a connection; he is more interested to know whether YOU know. Skip the connection and get right down to business.

Umm, Well, Like

You want a few seconds to gather your thoughts? Take the few seconds without the fillers. These are just annoying to listen to and don't add value to what you are about to say.

I, Me and Myself

Sure, the interviewer wants to know more about you. But the more that he is interested in is the value that you can add to the company. Don't talk about incidents about yourself that don't serve the bigger picture- how can you help the company grow.

Also, don't take credit for accomplishments at the previous workplace alone. Sure, your input may have been paramount, but the chances are you did not singlehandedly accomplish a successful project. Talk about your role in the accomplishment, but give due credit. It would portray you as a team player.

Perfectionist

Everybody is a perfectionist until they aren't. Don't be that person. Until you really don't spend half an hour aligning your perfumes in their position every morning, don't talk about perfectionism.

Sure, Maybe

Is that a yes? Is that a no? Are you on board? These two words are like putting your foot on the door. You still aren't sure whether you want to go in or not. Well, the interviewer wants a proper answer. And these two words wouldn't cut it.

Stuff

You have been invited for an interview to answer specific questions about specific topics. Leave the stuff for another day. Resist the urge to continue stories with sentences like 'you know, stuff like that.' It's just random and vague and invaluable and wastage of extremely valuable time.

Sorry

We all end up using the word when we get nervous or get ourselves in an awkward situation. Wouldn't you rather just take a few seconds to compose yourself before saying something that would turn awkward? Sorry shows lack confidence when used out of context.

Swearing and Slang Language

You may feel the urge to get too comfortable during the interview. Feel like you are talking to one of your mates. But you aren't; and regardless of how informal the conversation is, do not use swear words or slang language with sexual or racial connotations. Also, avoid talking about any controversies that the company may be going through. If your research showed that your interviewer recently got divorced, don't bring it up. Keep the conversation focused on positive words and adjectives that glorify your accomplishments.

Chapter 18: General Culture Questions

Is punctuality important to you?

Punctuality is going to be a hugely important aspect to look at for potential hiring managers. When someone needs you at a certain time, then they are clearly going to expect you to adhere to the time agreed upon. When you can't be punctual, it might indicate that you can't be reliable in other ways as well.

I believe punctuality is very important. There are times that some accidents might happen, which is why I ensure to try and always give myself more time than I need. You never really know what could happen. Being on time is also important because I know I get frustrated when I'm waiting for someone who is late, so I ensure that I don't do that to other people.

What skills do you have that aren't at all related to your work-life? What are your biggest talents?

This is a question to see what skills you might possess outside of the workplace. Your answer will give insight into the kinds of things that are important to you, and what other talents you might bring that the person conducting the interview wasn't even looking for in the first place. It can add a little booster to your abilities, and you are showing that you are dedicated and valuable in ways not just related to your specific position. For example, you might be interviewing for a graphic design position, but you also reveal you are good at video editing as well. This could help increase your chances of your employer remembering you and your valuable skills. Here's what you might share in regard to this:

I actually have the ability to draw rather well and come up with funny or quick catchphrases. I have an attention to detail, so even though it wasn't in the job description, I could help with social media management and create interesting content to help draw people in.

How do you define success?

It is important to be thoughtful when answering the above question although it may appear simple. The interviewers want to know your priorities and things that motivate you and whether it is big paychecks. Also, the interviewer wants to know whether you take a more personal and individualistic approach to success.

The trick with this question is the word success. It is exceedingly subjective and even a properly thought response could be easily misinterpreted. You may want to sound ambitious but end up appearing that you are eyeing up the highest office in the company.

It is right to term the above question as broad and leave a lot of room. Thus, in responding to this question, one should give answers that are relatively unobjectionable. Define success in a manner that relates to the potential employer in line with what you have led from conversation and job description.

Such a response as Holding a high position, to instill my ideologies to the workforce so they can achieve more is not a suitable response. Rather you should stay job-oriented and specific. For instance, you could respond by stating, I define success by implementing my expertise and skills to the financial management goals this company has established to achieve efficiency and build on your existing success.

What is a strong value that you have that is only related to a working environment?

When we think of values, we might first think of religion, politics, or philosophy. You won't need to think of this for a question about your working values, however. They want to know what is important to you. How would you describe your work ethic? What is something that you always remind yourself when the going gets tough at work? This is another question specific to you, and there are a few ways you can answer. Here is one of them:

One value that's important to me is persistence. Sometimes things don't go as planned, and you might have moments of failure, but I always remind myself to try again. If something consistently is not working, then I'll look for a different way to solve the problem. The more I focus on getting back on my feet and continuing the fight, the easier it is to achieve my goals. Even if I fail nine times, the 10th time might be the time I succeed, so it's always important for me to continue on.

How well do you handle criticism? Do you think criticism is important?

Criticism is important because it is what helps us improve. Some people will struggle to handle criticism and think that it means someone is personally attacking them. This can create a hostile work environment. For this question, you will want to make sure that the person conducting the interview is aware that you understand the importance of criticism and that you will be able to handle it if someone gives you a talk while on the job.

This is a good response to this type of question:

I can handle constructive criticism and take it with an open ear. It's not always easy to hear the things I might have done wrong, but I understand the importance of appreciating this so I can grow into a better version of myself. I also think it's critical that we find ways to have open communication within the office so that we can all feel comfortable improving each other as a team.

What would a perfect day look like in your life?

Interviewers are going to be asking this because they want to get to know you on a more personal level. They want insight into what you are like as an average person. We all have these kinds of identities within ourselves where there is the fun version that might make inappropriate jokes, and then the professional version that feels most comfortable in a stiff suit and with a straight face. These two different identities are not what your employer will want, however. They want a unique person who is going to make their workplace improve overall. Show off your personality and be honest. If at the end of the day you were satisfied with what you might have done, then what is it that your perfect day consisted of?

I would say my perfect day involves first having a quiet morning and a big breakfast because I like to take time to myself. Then, I would accomplish something small, even if it's just folding laundry, as when I'm not working, I still enjoy doing something productive to make me feel good about myself. I would likely take some time to relax, maybe listen to music or watch something on TV. Depending on the day of the week maybe I'd go do a little window shopping and grab dinner, or perhaps I'd just stay in and have a movie night with a friend. My perfect day is one where I can experience something, no matter how small, that was a little different than what I did the day before.

What environment do you thrive in the most?

This is an important question because they'll use it to gauge whether or not you are going to do well in this particular working environment. Some people will not do so great in a fast-paced environment, and others need complete silence and alone-time if they want to get any work done. Try to be general with your response since you aren't aware of the situation and share your adaptability skills as well. You would want to consider stating something such as this:

I usually do best when I am in a collaborative and growing environment. I enjoy working independently, but it is always nice to have a support team to offer ideas when I need them and solutions when I might have an issue. I enjoy a fast-paced environment because it makes the time go faster, but I also like slower and calm moments so I can really focus on the details of my work. Changing environments keep things exciting and I'm adaptable to the many different types of ever-changing environments.

Can you perform well when you are in a high-pressure scenario?

There are going to be high-pressure scenarios in every work environment. Clearly, this task is going to be more important for a position like an ambulance driver rather than someone who might take down appointments at a spa. However, in even the most relaxing and casual jobs, you will still need to know how to handle a situation if things don't go completely as you expected. Here is something that will help to ensure that the person doing the interview knows that they can trust you when there might be a high-pressure situation:

I think I do well most of the time in these kinds of situations. Even when everything seems to be going wrong, I know how to take a step back and really find the right solution rather than letting myself become flustered. I have experience in helping calm people down and explaining the situation too so that others can feel the same way.

How technologically savvy are you?

Variations: How are you with X software? or What types of software are you familiar with?

If you are applying for a position that requires you to make use of new technology, you must come to the interview fully prepared. This means you need to have already learned the ropes regarding the kind of technology they use. Nowadays, you will find plenty of free video tutorials online on how to use these types of software, so invest some time into honing those skills. If you think you need more help, then you can sign up for a training course or ask a tech-savvy friend to tutor you.

Once you are equipped with the right know-how, you should then keep a mental list of all the software you can use well. You should also highly specific instances of when you used them.

I am quite skilled at using X software, especially when I was responsible for responding to client emails and over-the-phone queries. I am also familiar with Y program and I found it to be very useful when I had to design the company brochure a few months ago.

What is your preferred work style? Do you prefer working alone or as part of a team?

An employer asks this question to evaluate whether you will fit in well with the requirements of the job. Some job positions require one to work on their own while others require staff members to work together on a daily basis.

This question is an open-ended one for you to give your ideal work style and explain why you feel the way you do. It is wrong to mislead the employer, and it can also land you in an unhappy place if you are hired.

Working on a team may seem like the most obvious answer since, after all, collaboration is core to organizational goals achievement. Avoid saying plainly work in a team as this response may send a red flag to the employer by suggesting that you would not succeed working independently.

Further, avoid saying work alone as it may seem like you do not like people around you and you would not be willing to collaborate.

Rather, mention your preference but say that you are flexible. Remember to point out the positives on both sides. For instance, you could say, For the most part, I prefer to work independently in order to meet my deadlines, but I enjoy group work to spark new ideas, or I enjoy both working on a team and working alone. Based on the project at hand, I can enjoy brainstorming with my colleagues but I can also work independently and complete my tasks on time.

What would you do if your boss ordered you to do something that is against your values?

Variation: What if your manager asked you to do something that went against your principles?

The common response is by asking the interviewer to elaborate on what that something is, but the truth is that it is actually not the point. What matters more to the interviewer is that you are aware of, and want to uphold, the values of the organization. So what you can say instead, is to explain how you would handle the situation with the best interests of the organization in mind.

Of course, in reality, you would not really do anything that is against your principles. However, the chances of your principles being in line with that of the company are high, anyway.

First, I will compare the task that the boss wants me to do with the principles the organization upholds. If they are in line, then I would have to do it even if it is against my personal views. On the other hand, if the task goes against the best interests of the organization, then I would have to question him or her about it.

How often did you usually go on leave from work?

Variations: What is your sickness record like? or What is your absenteeism record like?

Interviewers dread to hire anyone who always goes to work late or who frequently takes a couple of days off due to some reason or other. Of course, this question is an easy one to answer if you have a really good record (with five or less sick leaves within the last few years, for instance).

But, if you have a colorful absenteeism or sickness record, then you need to be prepared to give a solid reason for that.

Make sure to emphasize that this issue has been solved and will not let you affect your performance and presence at work anymore. Never pretend that your record is not taint-free when it is, since it is all too easy for the company to pull it up.

Last year, I had to take two weeks off from work because I was diagnosed with Hepatitis C. However, I have completely recovered from that and now that I am healthy, I assure you that there will not be any problems like this anymore.

Have you ever faced an ethical dilemma, and what did you do?

There is only one wrong answer to this question: That you have never faced an ethical dilemma. This may indicate to the interviewer that you have no understanding of ethical values, because even children have been faced with a decision to fess up or cover up their actions. A previous coworker may have asked you to lie for them or a boss might have exaggerated numbers to meet goal. If you have not faced such an incident in the workplace, use one from college or personal life. Provide the interviewer with the facts without naming names or showing emotional responses to the story. Communicate the issue, why it was an ethical dilemma and what your action or response was.

Why have you not been working for so long?

In other words, the interviewers are asking why you have been out of work. The question shows that the interviewer is skeptical, which is always the case. You may feel that it is a daunting question due to its offensive nature. The hiring manager is implying such things as having an issue with your past employers, being distracted by other pursuits, lacking enough motivation to get a job, or not being skilled enough.

It is important to know that the question is designed to test your resilience. The best approach to take is to answer the intent of the question calmly and in a factual way. The interviewer wants an assurance from you that you possess initiative although you were unemployed. They want to see that the tenacity and drive that you hold will be translated well in the company goals. In answering the question, be accountable and do not complain about the job market, the industry, and the unemployment rate among other issues.

The best response herein would be to state that I have been active in my job search, and I keep my skills up to date through business networking groups, social media, and volunteering. The response shows someone who is active and excited to be part of the organization. Also, you may respond that I have been job hunting steadily and interviewing, but I wish to find the most fulfilling opportunity before I jump in and give it my all.

Chapter 19: During The Interview: Common Questions Part 2

As relayed in the previous chapters, some of the most important questions you will be asked have to do with opinion and behavior: these questions will likely make up the bulk of the interview and give you the opportunity to tell your various stories (as discussed in Chapter 4) highlighting both your experience (hard skills) and your expertise (soft skills). Hard skills are the technical and professional skills that are gained through specific education and training, while soft skills are the character attributes and personal qualities that a candidate brings with them to the position. Soft skills are also transferrable skills, appropriate in any workplace scenario, meaning that an employee with excellent soft skills is flexible and useful in almost any position. These skills are gained not through formal training, by and large, but via personal experience and self-awareness; soft skills demonstrate diversity and broadness of experience, as well as attention to detail and openness to others.

Many opinion questions will lead to a discussion of what you "like" or "dislike" about working styles or job preferences. These open-ended questions can be disconcertingly vague, so be sure that you have prepared a couple of specific examples of experiences in your past positions that were exceptionally positive and fulfilling, as well as examples of what didn't work as well for you. Again, remember to avoid the pitfalls of pointing accusatory fingers at others or dismissing particular ways of working as negative. You are here to present yourself in a positive light, so stay focused—even when asked what you might "dislike." Reflect on how you work best and run with that. Various areas in which you might focus are as follows: you might mention that you work quickly or efficiently with little error; this shows your style emphasizes speed and accuracy. You might talk about how your structure your day, which reveals that you like organization and routine or that you tackle tough projects first rather than last. You might discuss how much you prefer collaborative projects because you value a diversity of opinion and skill to create innovation. You might talk about how you work best if given a specific goal and deadline, then left to complete it on your own, which reveals strong organizational skills and self-direction. You might discuss that you prefer electronic communication to phone conversation because of its efficiency and precision; you can think through and answer more carefully in a written response than in verbal communication. All of these examples reveal something about your working style and, thus, how well you might fit into this company's culture. As with previous examples, always try to come up with specific examples and concrete descriptions to illuminate how your preferences affect your working style.

One of the most common—and potentially most dreaded—opinion questions is the alarmingly open-ended "tell me about yourself." This prompt encourages you to reveal something of your personality as well as professional strengths, often used as an icebreaker to allow both interviewer and candidate to settle into the interview. It is also a way in which the interviewer can gauge how quickly you think in a spontaneous atmosphere and allow you to show how comfortable you are in interpersonal communications. While it may not seem that you need to prepare for this question—after all, you know exactly who you are—it is important to anticipate the question and have some sort of prepared response. If you are thrown off by the question and have no particular idea of where you might focus, then you will inevitably get caught up in a rambling and/or irrelevant response that sets a wobbly tone for the rest of the interview. Instead, think about this question beforehand in light of the position to which you are applying, your relevant past experience and personality traits, and the company culture that you have researched. One simple way to prepare this kind of answer is to give a concise sketch of where you are now, personally and professionally, how you got there, and what you hope to accomplish in the future.

Oftentimes, behavioral questions, in contrast to opinion questions, will ask for a straightforward example of a time in which you did X. Not only do these kinds of questions give you a chance to highlight the kinds of hard skills you gained from educational or training experiences, but they offer a chance for you to emphasize the kinds of adaptable soft skills that you have used—and, presumably, will continue to use in the future—to handle various professional situations and personal challenges.

Behavioral questions will often be focused on problem-solving skills. Detailing a story in which you successfully confronted and eventually resolved a problem reveals a host of abilities that are applicable in virtually all workplace scenarios. Problem-solving includes a variety of soft skills that are necessary to professional success: the ability to analyze a situation showcases your ability to utilize logic and unbiased observation to generate possible responses to a specific issue. It also reveals your ability to evaluate which response will be most effective before implementing a coherent plan and assessing final results. When asked about how you solved a problem, use this formula to create a story regarding one specific instance at a previous workplace wherein you had to apply these important skills. Outline each element and formulate a concise and coherent answer, from identifying and analyzing the problem to generating and evaluating various responses. No matter what the position, problem-solving skills touch on virtually all of the most logical and significant of the so-called soft skills. This can allow you to prove that you are quick to respond and intelligent in your reaction.

Another kind of behavioral question that you might be asked to answer deals with goals: how do you show that you are goal-oriented; how do you specifically go about reaching goals. In the first case, your past behavior demonstrates that you are interested in and adept at striving towards productivity and success. In the second case, your story should outline specific and concrete steps that you undertook in order to reach the goals. These kinds of questions can take many forms: "give an example of a goal you set and how you achieved it"; "give an example of a goal that you failed to meet and why"; "why are goals important to your ability to perform?" These are just a few examples of how you might be asked to explain behavior that leads to achieving success and cultivating motivation. Prepare at least two examples of goals that you once had and met to varying degrees: you can showcase how you overcame obstacles or adversity to achieve your goals, for one example, or you can detail how you implement plans in a specific way to pave the way for your accomplishments. In any case, be sure to identify a specific goal that led to a concrete result, focusing on the kinds of skills that you needed in order to reach the goal. This might mean hard skills—you had to learn a new computer skill in order to reach the goal you set—or soft skills—you had to learn greater flexibility in order to overcome the obstacles presented before you can reach your goal. Ideally, you will able to detail both kinds of skills in showing that you are motivated by goals and—most importantly—able to demonstrate behavior that allows you to meet them.

Behavioral questions will also often involve a description of how you make decisions. Decision making is a key component of critical thinking overall and reveals an independent, well-informed, and decisive employee. For example, an interviewer might ask you simply how you make decisions in the workplace, and sometimes they will give you a particular scenario to work through. This requires preparation in terms of reviewing the concrete details of how you came to an important decision in a previous professional context. They might also ask if you have ever made a decision that was either unpopular or, ultimately, ineffective: this is another excellent opportunity to reveal that you are adept at adapting, regrouping, and overcoming obstacles. Remember that it is always best, to be honest and that revealing a negative experience can actually reveal some of your best qualities, should you frame the response in the right way. An unpopular decision might ultimately have led to a greater good (think about parenting in this context: what is "popular" to the kids might not be what is actually good for them, but in the long run, they understand it was for the best). A decision that proved a mistake is another way for you to show that you can learn from past behavior and modify your responses to be a better, more effective, and more well-rounded employee. Nobody is immune from making mistakes, and decision-making skills are complex skills honed over time; past behavior is both predictive of future results and of flexibility, the ability to learn from stumbles. Good decision-making skills indicate that a candidate is knowledgeable and authoritative.

Behavior questions will also ask you to reveal how you prioritize your work and organize your tasks. Your ability to prioritize says a lot about how valuable you can be as an employee, as well as exposes a lot about your decision-making skills (or, alas, the lack thereof). For example, imagine that you are a lawyer working on a number of cases at one time: how do you prioritize which case demands the most of your time? You could consider the relative fees that the law firm stands to make in each individual case, focusing your time on those cases which will generate the most revenue. Or, you could determine that the cases with the strongest chance of achieving the desired results (a win, a dismissal, a deal, whatever the desired outcome might be) deserve the largest portion of your time. Or, you could decide that the cases that are most deserving of social or financial justice should take up most of your workday, even if they aren't necessarily financially lucrative or boons to the firm's reputation. Or, you could determine that each case deserves an equal amount of time and prioritize each uniformly. None of these approaches is necessarily wrong or right: they simply reveal a mindset and a work style that you will undoubtedly reveal in your answer to your potential employee. As with any answer to any question in an interview, you will want to be honest with yourself and your future employer, but you must understand that if your methods are not compatible with the company culture, then you are probably not the best candidate for the job. Thus, it is worth your while both to do research on the company—is it concerned with statistics and rankings, or is it concerned with outcomes and client satisfaction— and to frame your answers with that in mind? Priorities are strong indicators of employee behavior in both positive and negative ways. Even if you have the best of intentions in mind, if your priorities do not connect with that of your supervisor or the company, then you are clearly not a good fit for the position. Likewise, if you have a difficult time prioritizing, seeing everything as equal, then you are sometimes unable to discern what is most important in terms of productivity or general results. If an employee feels that interpersonal interactions at work are coequal with time spent on projects, then a company might rightly conclude that their ability to prioritize is not in reasonable proportion. However, if an employee is able to manage a number of tasks with success and on deadline, then it reveals a superior ability to prioritize.

Most interviews will employ a number of opinions and behavioral questions, in addition to the basic credential and experience questions. Be prepared with some stories, as outlined in Chapter 4, but also read on for some specific ways in which you can prepare particular answers to specific types of questions.

Chapter 20: Questions Employers Ask

While interviewers dislike cliché answers, they do not keep away from asking cliché questions. Moreover, you are expected to give customized and innovative replies to these commonly asked questions. Some commonly asked questions include:

Tell me about yourself.

What are your objectives?

What do you consider being your most excellent qualities?

Can you state some of your weaknesses?

What propels you most?

Describe your perfect occupation?

Where would you like to be in five years? Ten years?

Describe a circumstance in which you perceived a potential issue as a challenge. What did you do?

Have you experienced issues coexisting with a previous teacher/boss/collaborator and how could you have been able to you handle it?

Tell me around a period when you concocted an imaginative answer for a provoking situation that you were confronting. What was the test? What parts did others play?

What sort of issues is disappointing to you? How would you manage those issues?

Define achievement. Characterize disappointment.

What are your diversions?

Of which achievements would you say you are generally pleased?

Do your evaluations precisely reflect your capability?

Were you monetarily in charge of any allotment of your school training?

Besides these, you can expect to be asked questions about your field or area of work. You must have well-thought of answers to these questions and a thorough knowledge about your field. Lastly, you may also be asked questions regarding the organization and industry, in general, to assess if you have done your homework.

Chapter 21: Know About Benefits

In India, the employee CTC includes various C &B components like:

Fixed Salary: It includes Basic, DA, HRA, Conveyance, City compensatory Allowance, Special Allowances, and Others

Variable Salary: It includes Performance based incentive, Sale based incentive and Profit based bonus.

Reimbursements: It includes reimbursement of conveyance, medical, telephone, Books and Periodicals, Educational Allowance, Leave Travel Allowance.

Contributions: It includes the benefits offered by the company like Provident Fund, ESI, Superannuation, Gratuity, Statutory Bonus, Medical Insurance, Accident Insurance, Leave encashment etc.

We discussed Compensation structure in the earlier pages. Now let us see in detail the Benefit components offered by an employer.

Employee Provident Fund (EPF): It is a statutory contribution made by employer (12% of Basic salary) against EPF. Up to a salary (Basic+DA) of Rs.15000, employer splits 12% into two parts. 3.67% for provident fund and 8.33% for pension fund. (Pension fund is restricted to a ceiling on 15000/- of basic wages). Deduction from employee (12% of Basic) is eligible for u/s 80c of Income tax act. [According to newspaper reports, many companies have defaulted in PF remittance, settlement and filing returns. There are instances of employer illegally deducting its share also from employee. Instead, it can restrict its contribution on PF/PS wages up to 15000/-.] Employee equally contributes to his PF fund.

Employee State Insurance Corporation (ESIC):

Employer contribution is 3.25% on earned gross of employee if gross monthly salary is up to 21000/-. Hence employer keeps it as part of Employee CTC. The employee can avail medical treatment for self, dependents; claim for sickness and maternity. Employee contribution is 0.75% on earned gross.

Gratuity: Gratuity is payable to employee (on separation) for loyalty upon completion of 5 years of continuous service (relaxed for death and permanent disability). It is a statutory liability of employer. [If employer show gratuity amount as part of CTC, it should pay even if he leaves before 5 years, but the Act does not permit. His annual pay declines and he is cheated. It is safer for employer not to include in the employee CTC.] For early goers, the accumulated amount has to be paid as Reward, Incentive.

Statutory Bonus: As per the Payment of Bonus Act (Amendment) Bill, 2015, it is paid to employees whose monthly basic salary is up to Rs 21000/-. Minimum bonus payable is 8.33% and maximum 20%, on Basic capped at Rs 7000/-. Employer shall keep it as a part of CTC. Anything above the bonus salary ceiling is paid as Ex-gratia. Bonus is usually calculated for the financial year period from April to Mar. Employee should have worked for atleast 30 days for minimum eligibility to qualify for Bonus during the accounting period.

Group Medical Insurance and Accident coverage: This cover includes medical and accidental insurance for employee welfare. So, the premium paid towards it is shown in employee CTC. In lieu of it, they pay Rs.1250/- towards medical expenses every month amounting to Rs.15000 per annum, as per the guidelines of Income tax Act.

Besides these, leave encashment, interest free personal loan, rewards, employer sponsored certification course, Employee Stock Option Plan, maternity pay, are some benefits attributed to employee retention.

Employee Engagement

Going by the title, don't mistake it for engagement or betrothal function of employee. It talks about the ways and methods of keeping the employees fully productive and engaged at work in order to achieve the objectives of the organisation.

Going by the definition as understood in HRM circle, **Engagement** is the degree to which employees are psychologically invested in the organisation and motivated to contribute to its success. Simply it is related to employee job satisfaction and factors affecting it. It has a direct impact on the BSC (Business Score card) of the organisation.

Recognition, appreciation, motivation, compensation, training, career development, accomplishment are some essential factors found to be the drivers of Employee engagement. It is found that the employee's engagement levels, behavioural pattern and performance potential vary appreciably with staff-managerial relationship.

Based on how they are engaged (full/moderate/low/nil), their behaviour pattern is exhibited as loyal or dissatisfied. If it is left unchecked over a period of time, it affects the overall performance. Simply speaking, it enables an employee to show full capability. It is at this point that employees should understand the concept of employee engagement. Managers are mainly responsible for it.

According to a survey done by Don MacPherson, Co-founder of modernsurvey, 'employees are 38 times more likely to be fully engaged when they know and understand the organizational values'. How true! But if it is carried out in India, this result might vary and show a lesser value of engagement.

If so, when does an employee become disinterested in job? What leads to be fully disengaged?

The symptoms of disengaged employees are as follows.

Complaining: Nothing good has happened to me and there is no use of working here. Others are better than I am.

Lack of enthusiasm: They are least excited about new projects. They work for the sake of attendance and salary. Eagerly they keep waiting for the weekend.

Doesn't help others: Hey Dude that is not my responsibility. Do it on your own. I am always busy with my module. Sorry!

Gossip makers: Eager to gossip nonsense about colleagues and managers. Try to destroy team morale, team dynamics, mentality and psychology of employees.

Liars: Go about spreading shady rumours of grapevine. Make up stories, keep the employees tense and create fear about future.

Know-it-all: Unwillingness to lend ears and show an egoistic face. Speak with 'don't care attitude' and 'I know all don't try to teach me.'

Leave me alone: Never mingle in team, always stand alone. Want to work independent and dislikes peer's intervention or collaboration.

Irresponsible: Never take any responsibility, late for work, excuses to extend deadlines. Throw the blame on somebody.

No initiatives: Bad employee wants to be an average team player but will not take own initiative to finish a task. He will be waiting to be told what to do next. Somebody should push him to the next step.

No questions to ask: Bad employee will not ask questions and has no quest for learning or getting trained.

Distracted: Often getting distracted to miss the focus of work. Commit mistakes, procrastinate and miss deadlines.

Not growing: They are not interested to go up the career ladder. Willing to settle down at safe zone and get saturated. They are not interested to invest in themselves.

Pollute culture: Try to pollute organisation culture and pull down the brand image. Try to disintegrate employees.

If employee engagement methods are properly implemented and monitored, employee attrition can be arrested. This would reduce the employee turnover to normal level.

I am sure this book will help you overcome the interview fear and make you fit to face questions with confidence and succeed. From an HR professional point of view, a candidate besides knowing about job interviews should also know the ongoing HR practices relevant to the career. Keep on learning throughout the career to upgrade your knowledge.

With growing demand for Make in India, Skill India and Digital India, let's hope that enormous employment opportunities will be created to lessen unemployment in the coming months. Effectively and judiciously, it leads to utilisation of human manpower to the welfare of the nation. When this is the situation, you have to gear up and dress up to the occasion.

A model questionnaire is provided in the next part. Try to answer the questions in your words that would suit your current status and applicability. Keep it ready for reference purpose.

Wishing you all the best!

Chapter 22: General Advice

Let's now look at some general advice for job interviews. These are points that should be incorporated throughout the Interview process listed in the previous chapters.

Speak Enthusiastically

It's good to be enthusiastic about things, especially when it comes to a job interview. You want the interviewer to see how excited you are for the new job and challenges that might await you. As a southerner, I practice speaking faster when I rehearse sales pitches.

Appearance

Look Better Than the Job You Are Applying For

Sitting on your bed and staring at your closet is not going to get you that job. No one really knows what to wear to interviews, but there is one simple rule I preach and live by. You have to dress better than the job you are applying for.

Unless the job is on a beach or in the Amazon Rain Forest, you will not land the job if you are dressed in a t-shirt and flip-flops. Whether you are applying to be a janitor or a new partner at a law firm, you have to dress well. What does this mean, you ask?

It means that the more professional you dress, the better. If you are deciding between a blazer and a leather jacket, the answer is always the blazer. Look your best, that is always the answer.

It should be obvious that you want to look good for the interview. Have you ever wanted to buy something from a man in shorts and mismatched boots? Of course not. Because those are warning signs. In the same way, they will not hire you if you do not dress appropriately. Put yourself in a consumer's position and imagine the person selling something to you wearing what you are planning to wear to the interview. Will you buy a new vacuum cleaner from them or do they look like they have taken some parts out of the machine to sell? If it's the latter, consider a wardrobe change.

For men, I recommend you be clean shaven. If you choose to wear a beard it should look well groomed.

For women I recommend dressing professionally in a manner that communicates "I get things done" rather than following the latest fashion trends. Remember, you should look good according to what the interviewers believe looks good, not what you believe looks good.

For both men and women try looking online for images of people in the job you are applying for. This should give you ideas on how to dress appropriately for your interview.

Ask intelligent Questions That Require Lengthier Responses

No one likes dumb questions that could have been learned from their website or social media. Rather, ask things that are not made clear on the internet and encourage lengthier responses. If your discovery questions can be answered with a yes or no response then they are not good questions. Ask them to elaborate and give some examples. Try not to ask yes/no questions.

Get the Interviewers Talking

Along with asking good questions, you need to get your interviewers talking. Be careful not to delve too deeply into their personal lives, but rather stick to work-related topics. Get them to talk about the boss if he isn't in the interview, have them elaborate about the company and what it is like to work there. Get them talking about the problems and fears regarding the company as well as the good parts. Ask them what their vision is for the company or for the department. Remember, try to uncover their felt need.

Be Confident

This might be the most important part as well as the most difficult. Carrying yourself with confidence might not seem easy, but it is a habit that can be developed. Of course, your answers to their questions are essential but the way you answer it is important as well. Avoid fidgeting or breaking eye-contact when you speak. Believe in your own abilities and show the interviewer as much. If you are confident in your answers, the interviewer will be confident in them as well.

Quantify Your Achievements

There is a difference between saying "in my last job I had a lot of responsibilities" and saying "my last job required my services in both project management and admin." Don't be afraid to list your responsibilities. Everyone can claim that they had to do a lot in their last job while the reality is that they sat behind a desk all day and played Minecraft on the computer. Listing it will give your interviewer notes to make and if they were to ask your previous employer about it, he can confirm. Your previous employer might not feel the need to mention everything himself if they ask what your achievements or responsibilities are; but if they are asked the question directly, it will jog their memory and they will confirm it.

Your achievements are important, don't downplay them.

Don't Be a Cliche

Do you see that stack of applications on the interviewer's desk? They are all "team players, hard workers, creative, responsible, and quick learners." The clichés are everywhere and if you want to stand out, you need to avoid them as much as possible. You have to choose better words to use for these attributes or maybe even avoid them entirely. You may not see it, but there are eyes inside of the interviewer's head rolling away whenever they read or hear about what a hard worker you are. Instead of saying "I'm a hard worker," consider replacing it with "I had many responsibilities and if I had to work late, I did. If I agree to do something, I will go out of my way to complete my part."

Practice Your Answers Before the Interview

There are few things as nerve-wracking as answering questions that you didn't prepare for. It is always important to prepare for any questions the interviewer may ask. Sit down in front of a mirror or even get a friend or family member to ask you the questions the interviewer will most likely ask. If you repeat and practice it enough, you will have note-worthy confidence in the interview.

Be Honest

Honesty is the best policy. Lying about what you are capable of doing is the worst possible thing you can do. They will hire you based on the benefits you promise to deliver. If you are lying about your abilities it will become known and this could cause your time at the company to be short and contentious.

Body Language Is Important

Don't slump, don't fidget, and always maintain eye-contact. This is a simple rule to live by in everyday life as well as the day of your interview. If you are slumping and fidgeting, you may come across as distant, distracted, and uninterested. You might do these things because you are nervous but to the person observing you, it seems like you are aloof. Sit upright – not unnaturally straight but enough to come across as engaging and interested. You are selling your services to this person, after all. You want to make the best impression possible. You want to seem interested in the job so make sure that you radiate that enthusiasm with your body language.

Make sure to spread your eye contact around to everyone in the room.

Conclusion

Practice makes perfect! As with doing anything, you really have to put in the time and effort to practice the art of interviewing either into the mirror with yourself or to your friends and family members. Be brutally honest to yourself because this is the time when you can make mistakes and still stand a chance to get that job. A few weeks before going to the interview, you will want to get started on researching what the company is about and the sort of questions you might get asked. Keep practicing and you will appear naturally confident on the big day.

You also have to understand that not every interview is going to result in a job offering. Yes, you will fail (unless you are REALLY skillful) and that is okay!

As long as you have presented your most authentic and capable self, you have done your best. Learn from your mistakes and right them in the next interview.

Remember that although not every interview will result in a job offer, they are another opportunity to get closer to finding your fit. Be yourself, keep hunting and good luck!

www.ingramcontent.com/pod-product-compliance
Lightning Source LLC
Chambersburg PA
CBHW072002070526
44583CB00015B/1296